CW00536770

Repentance

Repentance

Turning from sin to God

THOMAS BOSTON

INTRODUCTION BY J. I. PACKER

CHRISTIAN
HERITAGE

Scripture quotations are taken from the *King James Version*.

Introduction © J. I Packer 2005

© Christian Focus Publications, Ltd.

ISBN 978-1-84550-975-0

Published in 2005, reprinted in 2012
by
Christian Focus Publications
Geanies House, Fearn,
Ross-shire, IV20 1TW, Scotland, United Kingdom

Cover design
by
Paul Lewis

Printed by
Bell and Bain, Glasgow

All rights reserved. No part of this publication may be reproduced, stored
in a retrieval system, or transmitted, in any form, by any means, electronic,
mechanical, photocopying, recording or otherwise without the prior permission
of the publisher or a licence permitting restricted copying. In the U.K. such
licences are issued by the Copyright Licensing Agency, Saffron House, 6-10
Kirby Street, London, EC1 8TS. www.cla.co.uk

CONTENTS

FOREWORD

Thirty or forty took a pew that afternoon—a few more than usual. 'There's normally about twenty,' a lady told us, 'which is quite good. It's because there's only one service a month.'

The extras had come for the baptism of an infant. A few sang. Everyone laughed. To sing, you need to know the tunes, but anyone can chuckle when the minister cracks a joke.

He made his opening prayer: 'Gracious God, your thoughts are not our thoughts, nor are your ways our ways.' And, as if to prove his point: 'You look at the ugliest soul and see, still unstirred, the wings of an angel.'

Next came the baptism, and with it another prayer: 'Send your Holy Spirit upon us and upon this water.' On the pulpit canopy perched a symbolic white dove, grubby, lifeless, unstirred. A ten-minute sermon on Matthew 10 brought the comforting news that when Jesus said, 'I have not come to bring peace, but a sword,' he only meant Christians are 'a bit different'. None refused communion, though some took one element and not the other. 'I got Ribena,' cried a toddler.

A few metres away, a former minister rested in his grave. Two hundred and seventy three years had flown past since Ettrick laid him there, to wait until the day dawn. So what? Thomas Boston's day is done. It may seem so, but take a look at the Visitor's Book in Ettrick Church and you will see the names of people from all over the world. Inducted on the day that 'the two kingdoms of Scotland and England' became 'united into one kingdom by the name of Great Britain,' Boston lived in a world of horseback journeys, where the village blacksmith acted as dentist; yet half the population of the Netherlands, American scholars, and a handful of Scotsmen have trekked up this dead-end valley to see the place where, for twenty-five years, he preached and catechised, prayed and fasted.

On the pages that follow, you will find some of the sermons Mr Boston preached there between 1717 and 1728. When he arrived in 1707, he found the natives ungodly hypocrites—'censorious to a pitch...blessing and cursing proceeding out of the same mouth; praying persons, and praying in their families too, horrid swearers at times.' Fornications, adulteries, and allegations of rape disfigured a congregation he described as 'drenched in fleshy abominations'. Not the sort of minister to aim for a gradual turnaround, he therefore resolved to set himself 'directly against' particular sins. In the spring of 1708, a man suspected of adultery came face to face with this unflinching Thomas Boston:

> After the woman was brought to a confession, the adulterer stifly denied. Dealing with his conscience, I took one of the twins she had

brought forth, and holding it before his face, posed him with his being the father of it. Nevertheless he persisted in the denial though evidently under consternation, his moisture being visibly dried up in the struggle with his conscience. He being removed, I went out, and dealt with him privately; and having observed, that two of his children he had by his wife, had been removed by death, soon after, or about the time, in which, as was alleged, he begot those two adulterous ones, I told him, that it seemed to me, God had written his sin in that punishment. To which he answered, That indeed he himself thought so; and so confessed. Being called in again, he judicially confessed his guilt of adultery with that woman, and that he was the father of her twins.

Harsh though this may seem, Boston was not an unfeeling excoriator. He knew what it was to bury his own children. Before his first summer in Ettrick had ended, his son, Ebenezer, lay in the churchyard. When another was born in August 1708, with struggling faith, he dared to call this child his 'second Ebenezer'. But two months on, he watched the nails driving into the infant's coffin. 'I was so moved,' he said, 'that I had not kissed that precious dust, which I believed was united to Jesus Christ.' He felt an urge to draw the nails again, but restrained himself because someone was watching. Then measuring himself by the same standard as the father of those twins, he sought to understand why the Lord contended with him in this way, eventually drawing comfort from David's words: 'It was in my heart to build a house to the Lord.'

Did this heart-searching mean that he made simplistic connections between calamity and personal sin? Not according to the sermons in this book. 'Beware of harsh judging,' he says. Extraordinary troubles may befall those who are not extraordinary sinners, and rich mercies sometimes come wrapped in sore trials. At the same time, catastrophe may be the direct consequence of shameless rebellion. If we are not consumed, it is of the Lord's mercy. We cannot say, 'What have you done?'

When Thomas Boston preached on repentance, he wanted his congregation to think rightly about their trials. He aimed to unsettle unafflicted sinners and 'to impress the people with a sense of their need of Christ'. Twenty years after his confrontation with the father of those twins, the adultery of another married man 'occasioned' the sermons found in chapters six to nine of this book. 'The unhappy J___ A____' probably heard this message from the pulpit in June 1728:

> Think…what case you had been in, if God had struck you down, as he could, in the very act of your evil work; how you might have been beyond all hope and possibility of recovery. You owe your life to the slow method of providence; his patience exercised towards you has kept your soul back from the pit. Therefore repent, and go no farther on….God is giving you space to repent: do not trifle and dream it away, lest you repent when it is too late.

His preaching of repentance, however, was part of his consecutive doctrinal and experimental preaching, not just an appeal at the end of a 'gospel sermon'. Repentance is a saving grace, he taught, wrought by Word and Spirit, in the soul of a believer, who with a sense of sin, shame, and sorrow, turns from sin to God. It is not optional. God commands repentance; whoever disobeys will perish. Waste no time. Delay will cost you your life. 'Repentance is a flower rarely springing up from a deathbed.' Do not think yourself safe because God has been slow to punish your sins—the slower it is in coming, the sorer it will be, and once executed, the sentence cannot be reversed. This message, he applied to saints and sinners, young and old. Sometimes he took several weekends to cover one text, 'simply marking his manuscript with an 'X' where the sermon was to be resumed on the following week.'[1]

If Boston's preaching sounds strange to the enlightened evangelical ear, it could be for one of two reasons. The first is that his method of preaching is no longer widely favoured. In the world of twenty-first century English-speaking evangelicalism, most preachers would prefer to preach a series of sermons on Luke 1–24 than on Luke 13: 5. It is not easy to imagine the minister of Ettrick sitting comfortably at a modern day course on expository preaching. 'Look, Thomas,' someone would say, 'you're completely missing the point. Where in the world are you getting all this stuff about repentance? It just isn't in the text. You're not teaching the Bible, all you're doing is dumping a whole lot of systematic theology on your long-suffering people. Haven't you heard of *Heilsgeschichte?*[2] Has no one told you about biblical theology? Can't you hear the melody line of Luke's Gospel? Off you go; back to your horse, and ride into the sunset.'

So, should you read Thomas Boston, or send him packing? You may choose to handle the text of Scripture by a different method, you might prefer to hear larger units of text expounded, but surely he has something to teach preachers and hearers in the third millennium. Do you want to learn how to examine your heart and life for this evangelical grace of repentance? Boston teaches you how to do it. Is the memory of your youthful sins odious to you? He points you to the only Redeemer of God's elect. Are you longing for that holiness without which no one will see the Lord?

---

1   Philip Graham Ryken, *Thomas Boston as Preacher of the Fourfold State* (Edinburgh: Rutherford House, 1999), 41.

2   Salvation history.

He encourages you to follow hard on the heels of the fore-runner, even Jesus. Do you struggle to apply God's Word to all categories of hearer in your congregation? Thomas Boston sets a high example before you.

Perhaps the second reason that his preaching sounds a little odd is that many of us rarely hear this simple message: 'Unless you repent, you will all likewise perish.' And if we do not hear that message, we will almost certainly not hear the doctrine of repentance expanded upon, or woven into 'Bible teaching'. There could be many reasons for this: uncertainty about the nature of sin, hesitation over the doctrine of eternal punishment, fear of causing offence, or even the assumption that those sitting in the pews have all been there and done that.

Set aside the call to repent, and we ignore something that has been fundamental to true Christianity from the outset. Prophets preached it, apostles proclaimed it. Jesus commanded it while he walked on earth, and continues to do so as he walks among the golden lampstands. If the call to repent and believe the gospel be not heard, Jesus Christ the faithful witness is absent. Everyone who believes in him turns from sin to God. Anyone who does not turn, does not believe in him. No repentance, no Jesus.

Scripture makes an urgent call to repentance and church history will show that no church has ever flourished unless repentance has been a key element of the preaching. At the end of his ministry, Boston could say of his enlarged congregation, 'They are far more polished in their manner... and fewer scandals fall out among them.' Whether miners with tears making channels on their blackened faces as they listen to George Whitefield, or people at Pentecost cut to the heart and crying out, 'What shall we do?' no community, no church, no individual, has been renewed or revived without repentance.

Today, the pulpits of Scotland are largely filled by men, and even women, who do not preach that message—hirelings who shear the sheep, but never feed them. That is why in the place where Thomas Boston exercised a ministry that would affect Christians all over the world, there is only one service a month. Such situations, repeated all over Scotland and beyond, will change only if the Great Shepherd of the sheep strikes down the hirelings, or brings them to repentance, and sends men out proclaiming, 'Repent, and believe the gospel.'

But why, in a few words, should you read this book? Simply because, unless you repent, you will perish.

Philip S. Ross

INTRODUCTION

I

The Reformation brought to light many biblical realities that had long been overlaid by mistaken ideas and thus effectively hidden from view. The true nature of the Bible's own authority, for instance, and of justification by faith and salvation by grace and of the church and the sacraments, spring to mind. Repentance also is a case in point.

In the Middle Ages, repentance was equated with 'penance'—that is, confession of sins to a priest followed by absolution and the imposing of a disciplinary penalty for the sinner to undergo in order to signalise genuine sorrow. Nor was this the end of the matter; for a distinction was drawn between eternal guilt and temporal punishment, and the theory was that while absolution remitted the former, thus saving sinners from hell, they must yet spend time in purgatory after death enduring the latter. Indulgences, however, issued at the Pope's discretion and underwritten by the treasury of the saints' superabundant merits, would secure reduction of the purgatorial period, according to the terms in which they were drafted.

It was Luther's outraged challenge to the sale of a plenary indulgence that would keep the purchaser out of purgatory no matter what his sins were, and that could be bought for persons now in purgatory as their get-out-of-jail-free card, effective immediately, that triggered the Reformation movement across Western Europe. The first two of the ninety-five theses that Luther in his dual role as university professor of Bible and preaching pastor of the Wittenberg Castle Church congregation, posted on the church door on October 31st, 1517, were as follows:

1. When our Lord and Master Jesus Christ said, 'Repent' he wanted the entire life of believers to be one of penitence.
2. This word cannot be understood as referring to penance as a sacrament (that is, confession and satisfaction [the disciplinary penalty] as administered by the ministry of priests).

Luther's positive point, that repentance means whole-hearted turning or returning to God, and that the Christian life is and must be as truly a life of repentance as a life of faith, was to find full expression in Calvin's *Institutes* (III:3), in the weekly set services of the Anglican Prayer Book, in a classic sermon by John Bradford the martyr, in a widely read small book by the Elizabethan Reformed and devotional theologian William Perkins, and in many Puritan utterances after that, crowned perhaps by the declaration of Philip Henry, father of Matthew, that he hoped to carry his repentance up to the gates of heaven itself. As, however, Puritan attention focused increasingly on conversion and regeneration, Puritan emphasis was more and more laid on the initial repentance leading to the penitent life, and this is reflected in the *Westminster Confession's* chapter XV, 'Of Repentance unto Life.'

1. Repentance unto life is an evangelical grace, the doctrine whereof is to be preached by every minister of the Gospel, as well as that of faith in Christ.
2. By it, a sinner, out of the sight and sense not only of the danger, but also of the filthiness and odiousness of his sins, as contrary to the holy nature, and righteous law of God; and upon the apprehension of his mercy in Christ to such as are penitent, so grieves for, and hates his sins, as to turn from them unto God, purposing and endeavouring to walk with him in all the ways of his commandments.
5. Men ought not to content themselves with a general repentance, but it is every man's duty to endeavour to repent of his particular sins, particularly.

In the book now before us, Thomas Boston (1676–1732), minister of Ettrick in south Scotland, inheritor and champion of Puritan theology and of the Reformational rethinking that preceded it, links together expositions first written for his pulpit on the necessity, nature and urgency of repentance, and the folly of ignoring or postponing this life-and-death issue. The sermons have all the qualities we associate with Boston: a dazzling mastery of the text and teaching of the Bible; a profound knowledge of the human heart; great thoroughness and clarity in exposition; great skill in applicatory searching of the conscience; and a pervasive sense of the wonder and glory of God's grace in Christ to such perverse sinners as ourselves. Proper appreciation of what we have here requires, however, some preparation of both head and heart, to take us into the world of Boston's wisdom, and I propose now to say something about that.

II

Flanking a main gate into what you might call Oxford's Mecca, an area containing the Clarendon Building, the

University's administrative centre; the Sheldonian Theatre, where degrees are conferred; the medieval Divinity School, and the world-famous Bodleian Library; pillars support sculptured heads of some of mankind's Big Brains. They are restored now, but when I was an undergraduate they had been weathered featureless and all you could tell as you looked at them was that they were meant to be human heads and not anything else. It is like that with the Bible-based, Puritan-ripened convictions about God and ourselves out of which Boston expounds and applies his texts. Modern thought has so weathered this faith that at first it seems to us a far-off and somewhat fuzzy historical oddity, not relevant for us at all.

Thus, Boston believes that the triune God, through whom we exist, in whose hands we are, and who will one day deal out our destiny, is *holy* in such a sense as to induce a sense of guilt and shame, unrighteousness and uncleanness, perversity and pollution, demerit and defilement, in all who realise His reality; and moreover is *sovereign* over everything in His world, even the free choices of human beings. But most today, while still acknowledging 'the one above' (or perhaps 'the man upstairs'), assume that God's nature is simply one of kindness without standards or expectations, and helpfulness that should shield everyone from harm all the time; or else they see him as an impersonal cosmic force, not *he* but *it*, making no difference to anyone, so that it is only common sense to live as if God did not exist.

Again, Boston believes that Jesus Christ, divine-human Lord and Mediator, our prophet, priest and king, crucified, risen, reigning and returning, offers himself in the gospel to everyone, inviting and commanding all who hear to receive and trust him as their Saviour, Master and Friend, through whom they may find forgiveness, acceptance and adoption into God's family, there to be transformed into the image of God's Son. Also, Boston believes that Jesus will one day be everyone's judge, and that everyone's destiny is either eternal heaven with Jesus or eternal hell without him. But most today think of Jesus as one more good man who taught and modelled decent behaviour, and they dismiss whatever most Christians believe about him as mere superstitious fancy. As for death, they conceive it as leading to either immediate happiness or immediate extinction, without Jesus being involved either way.

Again, Boston believes that the Bible is like a great illuminated circle, at the centre of which we stand with light shining on us from biblical teaching, narratives, biographies and circumstances to show us ourselves as we really are, and as God sees us, here and now; and he further believes that the Holy Spirit of God leads us to pass on ourselves the judgment that God passes, and to labour to change our ways accordingly—which is precisely what in Scripture *repentance* means. Thus, and only thus, to Boston's mind, do we learn what Paul meant when he said that all Scripture, being God-breathed, is 'profitable for teaching, for reproof, for correction, and for training in righteousness' (2 Tim. 3:16). But most today think of the Bible as at best a collection of ancient ideas about religion, some of which can still inspire but most of which are freaky and outdated, and all of which need to be relativised, in our world of multiple cultures, both religious and secular, to whatever the consensus of the culture currently surrounding us happens to be. For reason is in the saddle, shaping religion, which it sees as essentially a human construct, and while reason thus rides and drives, biblical revelation is left behind in the ditch.

And finally, Boston believes that regeneration of heart by the Holy Spirit of God imparts a truly new-created life, of which the exercise of faith in Christ, the practice of repentance toward God, the humbling of one's heart, the upsurging of joy in the Lord and the overflow of active love to God in worshipful communion and to fellow-humans in self-denying service, along with passion to progress in all of this, are the direct expressions. But most today see religion as simply a crutch and a comfort for the struggling self, something that most of us can get on well without, and so the evangelical existence just described is dismissed as surely self-deceived and hypocritical.

The world of spiritual reality in which Boston's teaching about repentance is anchored is now before us, in outline at any rate, and it has to be said at once that unless we ourselves are inhabitants of that world, or at least are prepared to discover that we should be, we shall not appreciate him as the perceptive, profound, skilful, Spirit-taught physician of the soul that in fact he is. In his own day he was admired not simply as an accomplished biblical scholar, though he was all of that, but principally as a master pastor, whose *Fourfold State* circulated throughout Scotland as the ordinary person's vade-mecum on the path to heaven. Today, three centuries later, this man of God yet speaks to us in print, shining the searchlight of Scripture on our disordered lives and pleading with us to face and listen to God as He speaks to us through His servant on the various matters that Boston dealt with—here, the reality or otherwise of our 'repentance unto life.' Too businesslike to aim at elegance, Boston nonetheless achieves eloquence by his down-to-earth clarity of style, expository order, and skill in clinching each point by appropriate words from his Bible. And, as with some cheeses, you will find that the more you chew what he gives us, the stronger the flavour you get.

III

What sort of people do these sermons on repentance address? In a broad and basic sense, of course, like all Reformational, Puritan and authentic Evangelical sermons, they are declarations of truth about God that are truly messages for everybody. Everyone needs to be reminded, and believers love to be reminded, over and over again, of the reality of God's holiness, awesomeness, graciousness, faithfulness, justice, greatness and glory, and these themes must ever be primary and foundational in preaching, as in Boston they invariably are. In all his sermons, God— God omnipotent, omniscient, and omnipresent; God in Christ exercising both mercy and judgment; God who searches hearts and whose wheels grind slowly but grind exceedingly small—is, so to speak, the subject and human beings the predicate; Boston is God-centred, even, as is said of Jonathan Edwards, God-intoxicated, and his first concern as a preacher is that all of us at the receiving end should be the same. We today are so used to man-centred sermons, in which God appears only as does Jeeves in P. G. Wodehouse's farcical novels, to get people out of trouble, that for some of us adjusting to Boston's perspective is a major effort. But sermons, as such, are utterances on God's behalf to stop people sinning and bring them closer to God, so it is still proper to ask: who in particular are the people whom Boston is addressing?

There is no doubt as to how our question should be answered. Boston is reaching out to impenitent religious people, old and young, high and low, of two kinds: the self-satisfied and presumptuous, and the procrastinators, whom Boston describes as the slothful and pictures as spiritual sleepers. He seeks to explode the pride of the former and the apathy of the latter, and to lead both into the repentance that both need—'salvation-work', as he calls it. So first he explains that repentance is a matter of the heart, a lifetime's task, a gift of God's Spirit through God's Word, a change involving conviction, distress, faith in Christ, humiliation of heart, 'holy shame' and violent self-dislike, a confessing, renouncing, and turning from all one's sins as one knows them and a sincere, whole-hearted turning to God in total commitment to obedience henceforth and for ever. Then he deploys as motives to repentance the command and call of God, the killing effect of sin, the prospect of death and judgment, the agony of Christ, and the dishonour that sin does to God. Then he shows at length how delay in repenting, for whatever reason, must ruin the soul. Then he dwells on the condemned state of the impenitent, however friendly the providences surrounding them may seem, and pleads once again for serious personal repentance on the part of everyone. Pursuing this story-line, as we may call it, he scatters incidentally a great deal of wisdom about the ways of God, as he regularly does in all his practical writing. To readers who are on his wavelength, he has much to give. But the wavelength question, I recognise, is a real one. There are many professed believers today whose sincerity and zeal are great but whose Christian reading has so far stopped short at what I would call Christian froth (of which, be it said, there is nowadays no shortage), and if Boston falls into their hands they may well be tempted after the first few pages to give up, feeling that this is tough stuff, old-fashioned and dry, and is doing nothing for them. Granted, Boston, like others of the sermon-publishing Puritan school, is something of an acquired taste; but to any thus stymied who turn back to this Introduction in puzzlement as to why Boston's book should be rated a classic, I say—keep going, I beg you; and have a ballpoint handy, to jot down Boston's headings as you come to them; and take note of everything he tells you about God; and when you have struggled to the end, go back and read the book again; and I guarantee that you will realise you have not been wasting your time.

Before me, as I write, is a leaflet announcing a conference retreat under the title: 'Repentance as the Way to a Blessed Life in the 21st Century.' The title declares a truth, and Boston can lead us into that blessed life as sure-footedly as anyone. So read well, think and pray about what you read, and God bless you through the perennial wisdom that His servant unfolds.

J. I. Packer

1

The Necessity of Repentance

(Several sermons preached at Ettrick in 1717)

I tell you, no: but unless you repent,
you will all likewise perish.

Luke 13: 5

When we consider the abounding sin and hardness of heart prevailing under a preached gospel, it must needs let us see, that the doctrine of repentance is both necessary and seasonable, to pluck the brands out of the burning; or if that will not do, to leave men without excuse. Sinners stave off repentance, as if they were resolved to persist in sin come what will, or at least as halting between two opinions. But here is a peremptory decision of the case in this text, 'I tell you, no: but unless you repent, you will all likewise perish.' In these words we have two things:

An abuse of a dispensation of providence corrected: 'I tell you, no.' Some had told our Lord the news of Pilate the Roman governor's falling on some Galileans, with his soldiers, and killing them, while they were sacrificing. It seems the tellers of this news, or others in the company, were apt to think, that these were sinners beyond others, because an unordinary judgment had fallen on them. Our Lord tells them, that it would not bear such a conclusion.

He puts them in mind of another remarkable providence, namely the tower of Siloam in Jerusalem, its falling on and killing eighteen persons: but here he shows that this did not befall them because they were greater sinners than all the rest in Jerusalem; no, there were as great sinners as those which missed that stroke, and others like it too.

The right use of the dispensation instructed: 'But unless you repent, you will all likewise perish.' The right use is to learn repentance from the ruin of others; if others give us an example at their own cost, that we take heed to it and improve it to our repentance and reformation. This is the import of the particle *but*.

An Authoritative Declaration

These words are a peremptory certification given to sinners by our Lord. And the proposition in its own nature includes a twofold certification.

A certification of ruin upon impenitence. Sinners go on in their course, yet hope that all may be well. No, says our Lord, deceive not yourselves; for if you do not repent, there is no hope of saving you. There is here:

1. The matter on which the certification is given, 'Unless you repent'. If you do not repent, if you be not duly humbled for your sins, and sincerely turn from them. If you harden your hearts under your guilt, keep still your sinful courses, and refuse to let them go, they will ruin you.

2. The thing certified, which is perishing likewise; not perishing in that very manner, but you will perish as surely as they did. The judgments of God will pursue you, and you will perish for ever.

3. The extent of the certification, 'all perish.' This clears the perishing to be meant of everlasting death. Though signal temporal judgments do pursue all that are impenitent, yet eternal punishment will; no

impenitent sinner shall escape that, however they may escape temporal strokes of signal vengeance.

4. The peremptoriness of it. This appears in two things: (a) That solemn assertion, 'I tell you,' supposed to be repeated in the last clause. Take it out of the mouth of the Lord himself, that you will perish unless you repent. This has been told you by many, but you would not believe: but now I tell it you out of my own mouth. And to hear this out of the mouth of the Saviour, may strike a sinner with concern, and let him see, that Christ's blood will never be laid out on a person continuing impenitent, to save him from death. (b) In the intimate relation to be between the punishment of those so signally smitten by the hand of God, and the future punishment of all impenitent sinners; the former is a pledge of the latter. This is intimated by the particle *likewise*.

A certification of life and repentance. This is implied here as Genesis 2:17. God has made as sure connection between repentance and life, as between impenitence and death. Be your sins ever so great, if you repent of them, and turn from them, they will never be your ruin.

Before I come to the main point I design, I will lay before you some observations from the words.

Calamity not the Measure of a Sinner

Those who meet with more signal strokes than others, are not therefore, nor are to be accounted greater sinners than others. The Lord spares some as great sinners, as he signally punishes: 'I tell you, no.' What are the reasons of this dispensation of providence?

God's sovereign power and absolute dominion, which he will have the world to understand: 'Is it not lawful for me to do what I will with my own?' (Matt. 20: 15). Thus our Lord accounts for the dispensation of the man's being born blind (John 9: 3). All men have that in them and about them, which may make them liable to the heaviest strokes that any of the children of men meet with. Therefore whatever any suffer, the Lord does them no wrong, since he punishes them less than their iniquity deserves. But amongst many whom justice may strike, sovereignty picks out some, and causes them to smart. And who may say, 'What are you doing?'

We are now under the mixed dispensation of providence; not the unmixed, reserved to another world, when all men will be put into their unalterable state. Now this is very agreeable that God signally punish some of a society, while others as guilty do escape, that the whole may, with David, 'sing of mercy and judgment too' (Ps. 101:1). And thus the dispensation of divers colours is held up in the world, as a display of the manifold wisdom of God.

The mercy of God to some is magnified by his severity on others. As black set by white makes the white appear the better; so God's severity against some, may be a looking-glass to others, in which they may see how much they stand obliged to free grace and mercy (Rom. 11:22). Men are never fairer to prize health in themselves, than when they see others tossed on sick beds; nor to prize the exercise of sense and reason, and other mercies, than when they see what miserable and pitiful sights they are that are deprived of these. And this should make folk patient and thankful under the strokes of the Lord's hand, because if he take away a mercy, health for instance, or perhaps a member or limb of their body, being taken away, it may be more serviceable for him, than when they had it, in so far as it will serve to magnify the mercy of God to others, that see and notice the hand of the Lord (see Matt. 21:3).

In very signal strokes very signal mercies may be wrapped up. So it was in Joseph's case; there was a very singular blessing on the head of him that was separated from his brethren. Job's troubles were but a dark hour before a very glorious day. The halt Jacob got in his thigh, was more excellent, as a badge of his wrestling with the angel, than Esau's retinue of four hundred men.

This dispensation is in some sort necessary to confirm us in the belief of the judgment of the great day. God punishes some remarkably, that the world may see that there is a God that judges on the earth; he does not so punish all, that men may be assured that there is a judgment to come. If none were punished here, the world would improve that for atheism; if all were punished, it would be improved to Sadducism.

Then learn that unordinary strokes may befall those that are not unordinary sinners; and therefore be not rash in your judgment concerning the strokes that others meet with. It is true, whatever we or others meet with, it is deserved at the Lord's hand; and when God follows an unordinary seen sin with an unordinary judgment, as in the case of Korah, Dathan, and Abiram, it is no breach of charity to judge that the stroke comes for that sin. But when people, in whose conversation you see no signal sin, meet with signal strokes, beware of harsh judging. For in the way of the Lord's dispensation, some will meet with a signal stroke for some sin, such as the world would think little or nothing of, if they knew it.

Then adore the mercy of God to you, and wonder at his sparing you, when you see others smart under the hand of God, which you do not feel. Acknowledge, that whatever others meet with, the same might have been your lot, if the Lord had dealt with you as you deserve; as the church did, 'It is of the Lord's mercies that we are not consumed, because his compassions fail not' (Lam. 3:22).

A Bad Forecast in Every Disaster

The strokes which any meet with, are pledges of ruin to impenitent sinners. But, 'Unless you repent, you will all likewise perish.'

They show how hateful to God sin is, in whoever it is: 'Who gave Jacob for a spoil, and Israel to the robbers? Did not the Lord, he against whom we have sinned? For they would not walk in his ways, neither were they obedient to his law' (Isa. 42:24). God has no delight in the misery of his own creatures (Ezek. 18:23). He must therefore have a mighty hatred against sin, in that he is so heavy oftentimes on the work of his own hands for it. Not only his enemies smart for sin, but his dear friends; yea, his dear Son smarted for it, when it lay on him but by imputation. And therefore how can impenitent sinners think to escape? 'For if they do these things in a green tree, what will be done in the dry?' (Luke 23:31).

They show how just God is. He is the Judge of all the earth, and cannot but do right (Gen. 18:25). Though justice may delay the punishment of one longer than another, yet it will not allow to punish some, and for ever to spare others, in the same state. For that would be manifest partiality, which God hates (Ezek. 18:20). Therefore the apostle tells us that 'it is a righteous thing with God to repay with tribulation those who trouble' the saints (2 Thess. 1:6).

Whatever any meet with in the way of sin, is really designed for warning to others, as is clear from the text (see 1 Cor. 10:11-12). And they that will not be taught by the example of others, may expect to be made examples to teach others, as Lot's wife was. But the wise will have their eyes in their head, while impenitent sinners pass on and perish, as those that will not take warning. Hence it comes to pass, that the stroke afar off not prevailing, is oftentimes brought nearer home.

All those strokes which sinners meet with in this life, are the spittings of the shower of wrath that abides the impenitent world, after which the full shower may certainly be looked for. As the joys in believing are the pledges of eternal joy, flowing from one fountain with it; the first-fruits of Canaan's land, which will be followed with the full harvest: so all the outlettings of God's wrath on sinners here, are the pledges of eternal wrath, and first-fruits of hell, which will be followed with the harvest of misery, being the same in kind (Rev. 20:14).

Be not unconcerned spectators of all the effects of God's anger for sin going abroad in the world; for your part and mine is deep in them. There is none of them but says to us, as in the same condemnation, 'Unless you repent, you will all likewise perish.' O how unconcernedly do many look on the miseries of others, how far are they from taking a lesson to themselves from them! But a hard heart and seared conscience, which cannot be awakened by the dispensations of providence far off from them, do but invite the heavy stroke to fall on themselves.

Consider, O impenitent sinners, how can you escape, when your ruin is insured by so many pledges of it from the Lord's hand, while you go on in sin? When a sinner goes out of God's way, he leaves his soul in pawn for his return by repentance; but the impenitent sinner never returns to loose his pawn, and so loses it. When God lets out any of his wrath in any measure on the children of men, that is God's pawn for his bringing eternal wrath on the impenitent; and we may be sure, that however careless we be of our pawns, God will not lose his. Therefore consider your ways, and repent.

Afflictions Observed Call us to Repent

The strokes that others meet with, are loud calls to us to repent. That is the language of all the afflicting providences which we see going on in the world.

God does not strike one for sin with a visible stroke, but with an eye to all. The reason which God gives in his law for punishing some transgressors severely is that 'all Israel might hear and fear, and do no such thing.' In the infancy of the Jewish church, he consumed Nadab and Abihu with fire (Lev. 10:2 cf. v. 9). In the infancy of the Christian church, Ananias and Sapphira were struck dead for a lie. Why all this, but to be a warning to all that should come after?

By that we may see how dangerous a thing sin is to be harboured; and if we will look inward, we may ever see, that there is sin in us also against the God of Israel. If we saw one stung by a serpent which he had taken up, would not we quickly throw away one which we had taken up too, lest we should fare no better? How can we think to prosper in that way, where we see it goes so very ill with others?

We may see that none go on impenitently in a sinful course, but over the belly of thousands of calls from providence to repent, besides all those they have from the word. Look out into the world, O sinner, and consider how many have fallen into ruin, and are still falling by their iniquity. As many as there are of these, so many mouths are there calling you to repent, and turn from your sin. 'Who did ever harden himself against God, and prosper?' Do you think, that your case will be an exception to the general rule? No; so many witnesses give their testimony to you, that 'unless you repent, you will likewise perish.'

Impenitency under the gospel cannot have the least shadow of excuse. The calls of providence common to the whole world, are sufficient to leave the heathen without excuse (Rom. 1:20). How much more will the calls of the word and providence too make us inexcusable, if we do not repent? Sinners make many shifts for themselves, to preserve the life of their lusts, and to keep themselves from this unpleasant exercise, but they will be fig-leaf covers before the Lord. How much more do strokes from the hand of the Lord on ourselves call us to repent?

> Therefore behold, I will hedge up
> your way with thorns,
> and make a wall,
> that she will not find her paths.
> She will follow after her lovers,
> but she will not overtake them; and she will seek them,
> but will not find them:
> Then will she say,
> I will go and return
> to my first husband,
> for then was it better with me than now.
> (Hosea 2:6-7)

What Absalom's design was in burning Joab's corn-field, is the design of afflicting providences. And therefore impenitency and hardness of heart under the strokes of the Lord's hand, are highly aggravated (Jer. 5:3). Every cross that we meet with is a charge from heaven to turn from our sinful course and from the particular ills of our way.

I come now to the principal doctrine of the text: Sinners, except they repent, shall perish. This is an except without any exception. Be who they will, if they be sinners, they must repent or perish. All are sinners, and by sin depart from God; and they must come back again to him by repentance, else they are for ever ruined. Be they sinners of a greater or lesser size, they must be penitent sinners, or it had been better for them they had never been born.

What Is Repentance?

Repentance is, in its general nature, a saving grace: 'In meekness instructing those that oppose themselves; if God perhaps will give them repentance to the acknowledging of the truth' (2 Tim. 2:25). It is a grace given us of God freely, enabling and disposing a soul to all the acts of turning from sin to God; and it is saving, as in its own nature distinguishing a man from a hypocrite, and having a sure connection with eternal salvation.

An Abiding Grace

It is not a transient action, as Papists and some ignorant creatures imagine, as if a sigh for sin, an act of sorrow for it, a confession of it with a 'God be merciful to me a sinner,' were repentance. No, no; these may be acts of repentance while they proceed from a truly penitent heart. But repentance itself is not a passing act, but an abiding grace (Zech. 12:10); a continuing frame and disposition of the soul; a principle lying deep in the heart, disposing a man to mourn for and turn from sin on all occasions.

A Wound that Bleeds till Glory

It is not a passing work of the first days of one's religion, as some professors take it to be; but a grace in the heart, setting one to an answerable working all the days of his life. It is a spring of waters of sorrow in the heart for sin, which will spring up there while sin is here, though sometimes through hardness of heart it may be stopped for a while. They that look on repentance as the first stage in the way to heaven, and looking back to the sorrowful hours which they had when the Lord first began to deal with them, reckon that they have passed the first stage, are in a dangerous condition. And whoever endeavours not to carry on their repentance, I doubt if they ever at all repented yet. As when Moses had smote the rock in the wilderness, and the waters began to gush out, those waters ran (it is thought, 1 Cor. 10:4) and followed them while in the wilderness: so the heart first smitten with repentance for sin at the soul's first conversion to God, the wound still bleeds, and is never bound up to bleed no more, till the band of glory be put about it in heaven (Rev. 21:4).

Hence initial and progressive repentance, though the former be the repentance of a sinner, the latter of a saint, are no more different kinds of repentance, than the soul's virgin love to Christ, and their love to him through the course of their spiritual marriage with him; or than faith in its first, and after actings. But as the midday and evening sun are the same with the morning sun, so are these; though the rising morning sun may be most noticed by the traveller, who having travelled in the night, was thereby brought from darkness to light.

No Common Grace

It is not a common grace, but a special saving one. Men may have a repentance for their sin, gnawing their consciences, and tormenting their hearts, which

> 'The stony heart may be broken in a thousand pieces, while yet every piece remains a stone.'

they will carry on in hell through eternity: being only the first movings of the worm in the soul that never dies: as Judas's repentance seems to have been Simon Magus's and Pharaoh's. They may bitterly rue their sin, as Esau (Gen. 27:34), who never truly repent of it (Heb. 12:17); and the stony heart may be broken in a thousand pieces, while yet every piece remains a stone. They may have a superficial sorrow for sin, and a light joy succeeding it, whose hearts were never pierced to the quick; and therefore the joy goes, as the effects of a send of rain on the parched ground (Matt. 13:20-21). But true repentance is a repentance never repented of, kindly working in the soul.

How is Repentance Produced in the Soul?

We may consider how repentance is wrought in the soul. Two questions must be answered and two points cleared.

By the Spirit

Who works repentance, or is the author of it? And that is the sanctifying Spirit of Jesus Christ:

> And I will pour upon the house of David, and upon the inhabitants of Jerusalem, the spirit of grace and of supplications, and they will look upon me whom they have pierced, and they will mourn for him, as one mourns for his only son, and will be in bitterness for him, as one that is in bitterness for his first-born. (Zech. 12:10)

Sometimes notorious prodigals become true penitents; as persecuting Saul turned to be a preaching Paul: so that the world is amazed with the change, and are ready to say as in Saul's case, 'What is this that is come to the son of Kish? Is Saul also among the prophets?' (1 Sam. 10:11). But that query, 'But who is their father?' (v. 12) gives a rational account of the matter. All sort of timber to divine grace is alike easy to hew. And forasmuch as the house of God is ordinarily built of the knottiest wood, publicans and harlots entering into

The Necessity of Repentance

the kingdom of God before Scribes and Pharisees, it may plainly appear, that repentance is not the work of nature, but of grace; not of men's own spirit, but Christ's Spirit.

This is evident from the word, 'Can the Ethiopian change his skin, or the leopard his spots? Then may you also do good, that are accustomed to do evil' (Jer. 13:23). It is the Lord's own work to 'take away the stony heart, and give an heart of flesh' (Ezek. 36:26). It is the office of the exalted Mediator to give repentance, in whose hand it is to send the Spirit (Acts 5:31). Ministers may preach repentance, but cannot work it in themselves, and far less in others. They may sow the seed, but cannot make it grow (1 Cor. 3:6-7). It is but a peradventure if God gives repentance, when they have done their utmost (2 Tim. 2:25). But if at all their weapons be mighty, it is through God (2 Cor. 10:4).

Through the Word

By what means does the Spirit work repentance? That is by the word, whether read or preached. The word is the channel in which the influences of the Spirit flow; and from these it has its piercing, melting, and heart-softening virtue, as the pool of Bethesda had its healing virtue from the angel's troubling water: 'And some of them were men of Cyprus, and Cyrene, which when they were come to Antioch, spoke to the Grecians, preaching the Lord Jesus. And the hand of the Lord was with them: and a great number believed, and turned to the Lord' (Acts 11:20-21). Junius, who was deeply plunged in Atheism, was brought to repentance by reading John 1 in a New Testament which his father had purposely laid down in his chamber, if perhaps he might take it up and read it. Augustine was converted by reading Romans 13:13-14: 'Let us walk honestly as in the day; not in rioting and drunkenness, not in chambering and wantonness, not in strife and envying. But put you on the Lord Jesus Christ, and make no provision for the flesh, to fulfil the lusts thereof.' Three thousand we find were wrought on by one sermon (Acts 2).

Many and various are the occasions of repentance, which the Lord blesses for bringing home the word to the soul, and the soul by it to God. Personal afflictions have been so in the case of many (Hosea 2:7). The sight of strokes on others has been blessed to some. The first occasion of Luther's turning serious was a fright by the violent death of a dear companion of his. No, God has made falls into gross sins occasions of repentance to many, of which there are several instances, as Achan, the thief on the cross, Flavel gives an account of one, in the case of an attempt of self-murder. Augustine heard a voice, saying, 'Take up, and read.' No, God can make a dream in the night such an occasion (Job 33:15-16). But these are not properly the means, but the occasions which bring men to consider of the word, which is the true and proper means. And here the Spirit of the Lord makes use of both parts of the word.

The law breaks the hard heart

'Is not my word like a hammer that breaks the rock in pieces? says the Lord' (Jer. 23:29). It goes before like John the Baptist to prepare the way of the Lord into the heart. And the Spirit of the Lord making use of it in a soul, is called 'the Spirit of bondage' (Rom. 8:15). And here each part of the law has its proper use.

The commands, to convince the soul of sin: 'I had not known sin,' says the apostle, 'but by the law: for I had not known lust, except the law had said, You shall not covet'

from, more than he can go out of himself. He must stay and answer, unless he prevail with the judge to let fall the process; as many do by silencing their consciences one way or other to their own ruin.

In this court, the Spirit of the Lord, *awakening the sleepy conscience*, sets it upon the bench, so that the man becomes his own judge: 'And when he [the Comforter] is come, he will reprove the world of sin, and of righteousness, and of judgment' (John 16:8). The man searches and tries his own heart and life, which was before neglected as the sluggard's garden. But now every corner thereof is ransacked, and secret things set in the light.

The man is convicted as a sinner by the law. His nature, heart, and life brought to the holy law and compared with it, he is found evidently to be guilty and a transgressor. Hence says the apostle, 'I was alive without the law once: but when the commandment came, sin revived, and I died' (Rom. 7:9). The law as a looking-glass is held before his eyes, and he sees his spots. His own conscience is as a thousand witnesses against him, and he cannot deny the charge. So his mouth is stopped, and his sin at length has found him out (Rom. 3:19).

The man is sentenced and condemned by his own conscience according to the law, adjudging him liable to death, eternal death, for his sins: 'Cursed is every one that continues not in all things which are written in the book of the law to do them' (Gal. 3:10). He is therefore a condemned malefactor in his own eyes, by the sentence of the law pronounced against him.

What are the effects of this conviction?

A painful sense of sin; an affecting sight of it (Rom. 7:9). For now the sore is lanced; and they see those sins, and that in sin, which they saw not before; and their eyes affect their hearts. As when the sun shines into a house, the motes are discovered, which did not before appear: so is it here. And the sin which sat light on them before, becomes a burden too heavy for them to bear; for now they are roused out of their lethargy, and feel their sores. It is a burden on their spirits, which sinks them; on their backs, that bows them down; on their heads, which they are not able to discharge themselves of. Therefore the soul coming to Christ is represented as a man with a burden on him: 'Cast your burden upon the Lord, and he will sustain you' (Ps. 55:22). 'Take with you words, and turn to the Lord, say to him, Take away all iniquity' (Heb. Lift off iniquity as a burden (Hosea 14:2)).

Terror on their hearts: 'Put them in fear, O Lord; that the nations may know themselves to be but men' (Ps. 9:20). The convinced jailor, a man who wore a sword, falls trembling (Acts 16:29) for the terror of God is too high for the stoutest heart, that knows not what it is to fear the face of man. The soul that was fearless before, because blind to its own hazard, now that his eyes are opened, is *magor missabib* (Jer. 20:3). For what heart can be strong before an angry God, brandishing the sword of a fiery law over the conscience, which awakened, is the tenderest part of the man?

Legal sorrow for sin: 'Now when they heard this, they were pricked in their heart' (Acts 2:37). There are stounds of grief that go through their hearts like arrows (Ps. 45:5); and these are very piercing, 'The spirit of a man will sustain his infirmity; but a wounded spirit who can bear?' (Prov. 18:14). The man sees now that he has been murdering his own soul, and he groans out an elegy over his dead self; which is raised the higher, that he thought his soul was alive, when really it was dead. He calls himself fool and beast for doing as he did. But what is very sad, though his heart be rent in pieces for his sin, yet it is not rent from it. What grieves him thus, is purely selfish; his separation from God, without whom he sees he cannot be happy; and his liableness to his wrath and curse, which he sees will ruin him for ever to lie under.

A racking anxiety how to be delivered out of this state: 'Now when they heard this, they said, What will we do?' (Acts 2:37). And here many times fear and hope take their several turns in his anxious soul; sometimes hoping, sometimes desponding, like Jonah in the whale's belly, 'Then I said, I am cast out of your sight; yet I will look again toward your holy temple' (Jonah 2:4). Conviction of sin will make way for care into the most careless head, and will make folk bestow many thoughts on the neglected salvation, that used not to bestow one serious thought upon the business. And this care will swallow up all others, as that of a drowning man to save his life.

Using the Truth

> The unconvinced sinner is an impenitent sinner. Hearken you young ones, and old, that have lived at ease, and with a hale heart, in respect of your souls' state, all your days. They may sleep sound indeed, whom the devil is rocking in the cradle of a natural impenitent state. But you will get a wakening yet, either in time to bring you to repentance, or when time is gone, and there is no more place for repentance (Jer. 48:11-12). 'For unless you repent, you will perish.' Ah poor sinner, you were never yet in the next step to repentance. Your sore has not been lanced yet, therefore surely the filthy matter is never yet cast out by repentance.

47

> Convictions and legal qualms of conscience are not repentance: for they do not qualify the subject for it, and that in part only. These are very necessary things I have spoke of under this head; but they are but like the unripe fruit, which must be ripened by the work of the gospel on the heart, and brought to a perfection by the warm sun of gospel-influences, before he that has them can be accounted a penitent indeed. Or rather, they are like the blossoms which go before, and differ in kind from the fruit, which often fall off, and no fruit follows at all. Folk may have had these many days and years since, that never repented to this day (Hosea 6:4). The first-fruits of the second death may be mistaken by many for the pangs of the new birth. And therefore you that have had them consider well what issue they have had; for it is not enough to have been in them, but to have got right out of them. Wrong curing of some diseases, breeds others, that prove mortal to many. The right issue out of them lies in three things:

>> *Self-denial,* or unselfing of the soul, when the soul is shaken out of itself for justification and sanctification too: 'I have surely heard Ephraim bemoaning himself thus, You have chastised me, and I was chastised, as a bullock unaccustomed to the yoke: turn you me, and I will be turned; for you are the Lord my God' (Jer. 31:18). Compared with verse 19: 'Surely after that I was turned, I repented; and after that I was instructed. I smote upon my thigh: I was ashamed, yea, even confounded, because I did bear the reproach of my youth.' They see the heinousness of sin, and the corruption of their nature too, so as they conclude themselves utterly unable to help themselves in either of these points, and so come off from themselves.

>> *Faith,* or believing; in coming to Jesus Christ for all, in point of justification and sanctification too: 'Surely, will one say, in the Lord have I righteousness and strength' (Isa. 45:24). The soul being turned off its own bottom, comes and builds on him for what it wants, and looks to him for his blood and Spirit. Thus 'the law is a school-master to bring us to Christ, that we might be justified by faith' (Gal. 3:24. See Jer. 3:22-23).

>> *Repentance,* or a kindly melting of the heart for sin (Jer. 31:18; Zech. 12:10), as done against a gracious God, whom the heart is knit to in love. The soul comes from before the throne of justice, where it stood weeping for itself and its own misery, to the throne of grace, where it stands weeping for having offended such a gracious Father.

They land at this threefold shore, who come rightly out of these depths. But many plunge up and down in them a while, and land again at the same side they went in:

>> *At the shore of formality,* or a legal walk: 'Having a form of godliness but denying the power thereof' (2 Tim. 3:5). They change their former ways but retain their old heart. They go indeed to religious duties, but they never go out of them to Christ. They act not as they did; but still they have the old principle of action, acting from self, and to self; so that though they change their work, they still work for the old master. And thus many continue in a profession of religion, living on their duties, never coming to Christ. Others land at the shore.

>> *At the shore of their former security.* They are neither better inwardly nor outwardly; but they come out of their qualms of conscience, as one out of a fever, returning just to their old way of living; as was the case with Felix, who said to Paul, 'Go your way for this time; when I have a convenient season, I will call for you' (Acts 24:25).

>> *At the shore of profanity;* turning worse than before: 'When the unclean spirit is gone out of a man, he walks through dry places, seeking rest, and finds none. Then he says, "I will return into my house from whence I came out," and when he is come, he finds it empty, swept, and garnished. Then goes he, and takes with himself seven other spirits more wicked than himself, and they enter in and dwell there: and the last state of that man is worse than the first' (Mat. 12:43-5). Their lusts dammed up for a while, run with more vigour than ever thereafter.

A Believing Soul

The soul in which repentance is wrought, is a believing soul. Faith is the spring and source of repentance so that though the grace of faith and repentance are given together and at once in respect of time, yet, in the order of nature, faith goes before repentance, and the acting of faith goes before the exercise of repentance. And he that would repent, must first believe in Christ that he may repent. I know that some teach otherwise. But this is the doctrine of the Scriptures and our Catechism.

Faith comes first

Faith is absolutely the leading grace, and the first breathing of a quickened soul: 'Without faith it is impossible to please God' (Heb. 11:6); therefore it is impossible to repent, for that is very pleasing to him (Jer. 31:20). So John 15:5, 'Without me,' that is, separate from me, and there is no union with him but by the Spirit of faith, 'you can do nothing' acceptable to God, therefore you cannot repent.

Faith leads to repentance

It is particularly the leading grace to repentance: 'They will look upon me whom they have pierced, and they will mourn for him, as one mourns for his only son' (Zech. 12:10). Thus it is represented in fact: 'And a great number believed, and turned to the Lord' (Acts 11:21). If repentance be the emptying of the soul by the dropping of the tears of godly sorrow, it is faith that generates them in the heart. It is faith that melts the hard heart, which drops in repentance. The eye of faith fixes on God in Christ, and then the soul turns to him by repentance (Jer. 3:22).

Scripture provides the motives

The Scripture usually proposes the objects of faith, and promises of grace, for motives to repentance; thereby discovering, that it is by a believing application of these, that a soul is brought to repentance: 'Turn, O backsliding children, says the Lord, for I am married to you' (Jer. 3:14). 'Return, you backsliding children, and I will heal your backslidings: behold, we come to you, for you are the Lord our God' (Jer. 3:22). 'Therefore also now, says the Lord, Turn you even to me with all your heart, and with fasting, and with weeping, and with mourning. And rend your heart and not your garments, and turn to the Lord your God: for he is gracious and merciful, slow to anger, and of great kindness, and repents him of the evil' (Joel 2:12-13). 'Come and let us return to the Lord: for he has torn, and he will heal us: he has smitten, and he will bind us up' (Hosea 6:1). 'O Israel, return to the Lord your God, for you have fallen by your iniquity' (Hosea 14:1). The very law proclaimed on Mount Sinai with so much terror, is graciously prefaced with gospel-grace for faith to work on in the first place; 'I am the Lord your God.' Thus the doctrine of the New Testament concerning repentance is proposed to sinners 'Repent for the kingdom of heaven is at hand' (Matt. 3:2; 4:17).

No repentance without Christ

The nature of repentance plainly teaches this. It is a cordial turning from sin to God: but is it possible to turn to God but through Christ? 'I am the way, and the truth, and the life: no man comes to the Father, but by me' (John 14:6). And is there any way of coming to Christ, but by faith? The soul, then, that would turn and go to God again by repentance, must needs take Christ by faith, by the way. The people indeed wept; but did they put away the strange wives, or set to it, till Shechaniah cried, 'We have trespassed against our God, and have taken strange wives, of the people of the land: yet now there is hope in Israel concerning this thing' (Ezra 10:2)? They must not be only prisoners of fear, but of hope that will turn, 'Turn you to the strong hold, you prisoners of hope' (Zech. 9:12).

Repentance is a kindly humiliation and mourning for sin; though the faithless heart may roar under law-horror, it will never kindly mourn but under gospel influences.

Why does Scripture sometimes put repentance first?

Repentance is placed before faith in Mark 1:15; and sometimes repentance only is mentioned to natural men as the way to salvation, as in our text, Acts 2:38, and 3:19.

Repentance no doubt is absolutely necessary to salvation; and no man needs pretend to faith, that does not repent, for they are inseparable. But that will no more infer the precedency of repentance to faith, than that Hebrews 12:14 will infer the precedency of holiness to it. Now, this is all that our text aims at.

Repentance being the end, and faith the means to that end, no wonder they be so placed: for the end is first in one's intention, yet the means are first in practice (so Mark 1:15). Christ commands sinners to repent; but then in order to repent, he commands them to believe. So in Acts 2:38, believing is implied in the command to be baptized. And therefore, speaking of the result of this work it is said, 'All that believed' (v. 44). So Acts 3:19 it is implied in being converted; compared with Hebrews 3:12: 'Take heed, brethren, lest there be in any one of you an evil heart of unbelief, in departing from the living God.' And that this is the true reason of this way of speaking, namely, that repentance is the end, and faith the means, is clear from Acts 20:21: 'Testifying—repentance toward God and faith toward our Lord Jesus Christ': for that Scripture can bear no other meaning, without destroying that fundamental truth, that Christ is the way to the Father. John preached repentance (Mark 1:4), but how did he direct them to it? 'John truly baptized with the baptism of repentance, saying to the people that they should believe on him which should come after him, that is, on Christ Jesus' (Acts 19:4).

Using the Truth

> It is not gospel-doctrine, that Christ will receive none but true penitents, or that none but such have a warrant to embrace Christ by faith: 'And the Spirit and the bride say, Come. And let him that hears say, Come. And let him that is thirsty, come: and whoever will, let him take the water of life freely.' The evil of this doctrine is, that it sets sinners to spin repentance out of their own bowels, and to fetch it with them to Christ, instead of coming to him by faith to get it. And it hinders sensible sinners from coming to Christ, as keeping them back till they be persuaded that they have true repentance. I say, persuaded; for how can a sinner come to Christ till he be persuaded he has a warrant so to do? If Christ will receive none but such as have true repentance, then none other are invited to come; for surely those that are invited, will be welcome upon their coming: if none other be invited, then impenitent sinners are not bound to come to Christ; for none are bound to come, but those that are invited; 'for where there is no law, there is no transgression.' However, none are here in Christ by faith, but whereupon they become true penitents; and none but true penitents will see heaven.

> Then for sensible sinners to think that they dare not and ought not to believe, and embrace Christ, till they be more deeply humbled, and do more thoroughly repent of their sins, and in a word, be more fit to receive him, is but a gilded deceit, and a trick of the false heart, to make the soul stay long in the place of the breaking forth of children, and die there at length. The Scripture holds forth quite another doctrine: 'Behold, I stand at the door, and knock; if any man hear my voice, and open the door, I will come in to him, and will sup with him, and he with me' (Rev. 3:20). 'Ho, every one that thirsts, come, buy and eat, yes, come, buy wine and milk without money and without price' (Isa. 55:1). It is one thing what a sinner will do; another, what he may and ought to do. It is very true, there are many who will never come to Christ, if they be not made more sensible of their need of him than they are. But all that hear the gospel may and ought to come, be their case what it will; and those that come not, will be condemned for their not coming (John 3:19). Therefore let every sensible sinner under that temptation think, that he is in the case of a drowning man, who if he stand disputing whether he may catch hold of the rope reached to him to haul him to land, a wave may come and sweep away; and therefore without disputing he must take hold of it.

> This shows the true way to deal with a hard heart, to soften it, and bring it to hearty repentance. It is to believe. You must do like these birds, that first fly up, and then come down on their prey; first soar aloft in the way of believing, and then come down in true humiliation: 'They shall look upon him they have pierced, and they shall mourn for him.' One may otherwise toil long in vain with a hard heart. Unbelief will lock up the heart, as the waters with hard frost; for hard thoughts of God set the soul at a distance more and more from him, when the believing of the proclaimed pardon touches the rebels' hearts, and makes them come in.

> The more faith, the more repentance; as the fuller the spring is, the streams run with more vigorous current. According to your faith be it unto you, is the rule of the dispensation of grace. For faith is the provisor for all other graces, as being the conduit pipe by which grace comes from the fountain of grace to the soul; so that it failing, all fails; and it moving vigorously, the rest do so too.

> *How are we to act in faith in order to gain repentance?*
Firmly believe, that whatever your guilt be, God is reconciled to you in Christ Jesus; that there is hope for your case, if you can attain to the way laid out for bettering it. You have God's word for this: 'Come now, and let us reason together, says the Lord: though your sins be as scarlet, they will be as white as snow; though they be red like crimson, they will be as wool' (Isa. 1:18). 'Have I any pleasure at all that the wicked should die? says the Lord God: and not that he should return from his ways and live?' (Ezek. 18:23). This will quicken your endeavours after the happiness of your souls. Satan strikes at this foundation, to keep the soul from repentance, many ways. He will tell you, it cannot be thought that God can ever love the like of you. But the Lord says the contrary: 'I will heal their backsliding, I will love them freely: for my anger is turned away from him' (Hosea 14:4). Again, Satan will tell you, that you were not elected, but made for destruction; though God never set him nor you in the secrets of his decrees: 'The secret things belong to the Lord our God: but those things which are revealed belong to us' (Deut. 29:29). But why does he tell you all this, but to make you careless? Which being done, he knows you cannot repent.

> Believe that Jesus Christ is both able and willing to save you from sin and from wrath. You have ground to believe his ability: 'The blood of Jesus Christ his Son cleanses us from all sin' (1 John 1:7). 'He is able to save them to the uttermost, that come to God by him, seeing he ever lives to make intercession for them' (Heb. 7:25). And you have also ground to believe his willingness (Isa. 55:1; Rev. 22:17). This will set you a step further; and truly this being believed by a sensible sinner, the bargain is almost closed. Therefore Satan works against the tossed soul's believing this, to the end he may not come to an anchor or rest, but may plunge up and down in the depths, knowing no landing place. Hence these hellish suggestions, What have you to do with the promises of grace? They will be made out to others, but not to you. But see Acts 2:39 compared with verse 36. Hence also the suggestion of having sinned the unpardonable sin. But why is that sin unpardonable? Not that the physician cannot or will not cure it (Heb. 7:25; John 6:37), but because the sinner will never after desire to come to him, but wilfully and maliciously rejects him. Hence also that suggestion, that Christ died not for him. But surely Satan never saw the roll of those whom Christ died for, and knows it no more than we (Deut. 29:29). We ought not to call that in question, but leave that matter to the Lord. It is plain, that we are commanded to believe (1 John 3:23). Let us do so, and we will have evidences that Christ died for us.

> This being done, believe that Christ is yours (Song 2:16); that God is reconciled to you in him; that your sins are pardoned for Christ's sake, and you are no more under condemnation for them (Rom. 8:1); that you are now in a state of peace with God, and safe under the covert of blood. This will effectually melt your hearts into sincere repentance. And the stronger your confidence be in this point, the fire will be the more keen to melt the soul. Satan will oppose you in this also, that raising the dust of doubts and fears, your hands may be feeble that should fight against your lusts, the legs weak and trembling wherewith you should turn from sin to God. But the more he weakens that, the more he serves his own purpose against you.

> Stand upon this shore, and look to your sins, and Saviour (Zech 12:10). When a soul has, by a believing application of the blood of Christ passed the gulf of condemnation and sees itself safe on the other side, it stands fairest for a hearty melting for sin, and a free and cordial turning from it to God (Luke 7:37-8 compared with v. 47). It is slavish fear that may be greater before, but it is filial relenting that will be greatest then. The waters of sorrow may make greater noise before, but they will come sweeping down with a more full flood then, as when a hearty thaw comes after a long frost.

> Believing the promise of his grace, use the means. There are means of God's appointment to stir up a soul to repentance; namely, serious meditations on the sins of our nature, heart, lip and life; the evil of it with respect to God, and to ourselves, 'Remember from whence you are fallen, and repent' (Rev. 2:5). 'I thought on my ways, and turned my feet to your testimonies' (Ps. 119:59). There are promises of repentance, 'Then will you remember your own evil ways, and your doings that were not good, and will loathe yourselves in your own sight, for your iniquities, and for your abominations' (Ezek. 36:31). 'Him has God exalted with his right hand to be a Prince and a Saviour, for to give repentance to Israel, and forgiveness of sins' (Acts 5:31). To believe the promise without use of the means is presumption; to use the means without believing the promise, is a selfish unsanctified work. What God has joined, either of these puts asunder, and so must be fruitless. God says to us in this case, as to Moses, 'Go on before the people, and take with you of the elders of Israel: and your rod with which you struck the river, take in your hand, and go. Behold, I will stand before you there upon the rock in Horeb; and you will smite the rock, and there will come water out of it, that the people may drink' (Exod. 17:5-6). The means are as the rock, the faith of the promise the rod of God: the way to get the water was by smiting the rock with the rod.

2

The Parts of Repentance

Let us consider the parts of repentance. These are two, namely, humiliation for sin, and turning from sin to God. These two put together, make up true repentance. Accordingly the Scripture speaks of those repenting of sin, 'which have not repented of the uncleanness' (2 Cor. 12:21) and likewise repenting from sin, 'not laying aside the foundation of repentance from dead works' (Heb. 6:1). So in the Old Testament repentance is expressed by two words; the one denoting remorse and sorrow, 'Wherefore I abhor myself, and repent in dust and ashes' (Job 42:6). 'No man repented him of his wickedness, saying, What have I done?' (Jer. 8:6); the other denoting the turning of the soul, namely from sin to God, 'Repent, and turn yourselves from all your transgressions' (Ezek. 18:30).

However these may be distinguished, they cannot be divided in true repentance. True humiliation issues always in turning; and turning always begins at humiliation. Hence very often the whole of repentance is expressed by returning, and sometimes by humiliation, 'If then their uncircumcised hearts be humbled, and they then accept the punishment of their iniquity' (Lev. 26:41); 'When he was in affliction, he sought the Lord his God, and humbled himself greatly before the God of his fathers' (2 Chron. 33:12). We have both together, 'Now therefore, says the Lord, turn to me with all your heart, and with fasting, and with weeping, and with mourning. And rend your heart and not your garments, and turn to the Lord your God: for he is gracious and merciful, slow to anger, and of great kindness, and he relents from doing harm' (Joel 2:12-13).

Humiliation

This leads the van in the sinner's return to God by repentance. There is never a soul comes back to God, but it comes the low way of humiliation. The sinner gone from God, is set up against him: but grace puts down the sinner from that seat, and

Humiliation
• A Sense of Sin
• Sorrow
• Shame
• Self-loathing
• Confession

lays him down at the Lord's footstool, where the Lord takes him up: 'Humble yourselves therefore under the mighty hand of God, that he may exalt you in due time' (1 Pet. 5:6). As it was with Benhadad's servants (1 Kings 20:31-2), so it is with the convinced sinner: faith teaches them, that the King of Israel is a merciful King; repentance girds sackcloth on their loins, and ropes on their heads, and in that posture brings them to him.

A Sense of Sin

A kindly sense of sin, whereby the soul sees and is deeply affected with its sins against a holy, gracious God. I call it so, to distinguish it from the legal convictions spoken of before, which make a terrible reel in the conscience and affections; whereas this kindly soaks into the heart. The former is at the bottom involuntary, comes in, and is kept on against the sinner's will; because the natural enmity of the heart against God is not broken; and makes the man like one under great pain, who would gladly sleep, but still the new stounds awake him, and keep him awake. The latter is voluntary, it is welcomed in, and welcome to stay; because the heart is brought low, and would gladly be lower before a holy God. When the light appears at a chink, they would fain draw the curtains, and open the windows, that they may get a better sight of their black face and foul hands (Jer. 3:18-19).

What the humbled sinner sees

The plague of the heart, or sin of the nature (1 Kings 8:38; Rom. 7:7-8). The man that is humbled, sees the corruption of his nature, himself to be a mass of corruption and confusion. He discerns the bias of his heart to the wrong side, the aversion to do good, the proneness to evil, that is interwoven with his very nature. The light of the Lord shining into his soul, gives him the affecting sight of the distortion and pravity that is in all the faculties of his soul, the blindness in his mind, rebellion in his will, and carnality in his affections. The want of this is a flaw in the repentance of many, of whom we may say, 'He is a leprous man, he is unclean: the priest will pronounce him utterly unclean, his plague is in his head' (Lev. 13:44). They never see the corruption of their nature, and so repent not of it.

Actual sins: 'Then he shows them their work, and their transgressions that they have exceeded' (Job 36:9). These are the poisonous streams flowing from the impoisoned fountain: 'For from within, out of the heart of men, proceed evil thoughts, adulteries, fornications, murders, thefts, covetousness, wickedness, deceit, lasciviousness, an evil eye, blasphemy, pride, foolishness' (Mark 7:21-22). Sin now lies at the door; for those things that were buried out of sight, have a resurrection, and stand before him as an exceeding great army which he has mustered against heaven. Sins committed many years before, will appear more fresh and green than that day they were committed. What he justified before as no faults, he will be now ashamed of; and what were reckoned tolerable follies, will be accounted monstrous impieties.

The particular idol of jealousy, which the man has been most apt to be led away with. The soul is never truly humbled, till deeply sensible of its weak side: 'Ashur will not save us, we will not ride upon horses, neither will we say any more to the work of our hands, You are our gods' (Hosea 14:3). For the penitent will be particularly set against that, as what is particularly offensive to God (Ps. 18:22). This right eye smarts and pains him so exceedingly, that now he would gladly have it plucked out. And as it especially grieves the Lord's Spirit, it specially grieves his, as what has been the great make-bate between God and him.

The numerousness and multitude of their sins: 'How many are my iniquities and sins? Make me to know my transgression and my sin' (Job 13:23). A true sense of sin will open men's eyes to see innumerable evils compassing them about, countable only by him who tells the stars (Ps. 19:12). Hence the humbled soul is sensible of a cloud of guilt that it has been wrapped up in; and will see it must plead guilty to every line of the spiritual law: sees itself a mass of iniquity; 'from the crown of the head to the sole of the foot, there is no soundness, but wounds, and bruises, and putrifying sores' (Isa. 1:6). 'We are all as an unclean thing, and all our righteousnesses are as filthy rags' (Isa. 64:6).

The heinousness of their sins, the aggravating circumstances wherewith they have been attended: 'I will arise, and go to my father, and will say to him, Father, I have sinned against heaven, and before you' (Luke 15:18). Each sin pierces the heart of the penitent. And so it is wonderful to see what a dexterity a repenting sinner has in aggravating his sins, in his prayers and complaints. Time, place, person, and each circumstance, shoot as it were a dart through the liver.

The evil of sin. Men may see sin, that see not the evil of it. Hence professing sin, instead of confessing it; turning to it, instead of turning from it. But if one saw the serpent's sting, he would not take it into his bosom (Luke 23:34). But the Lord's language to the soul whom he is drawing to repentance, is that, 'Your own wickedness will correct you, and your backsliding will reprove you: know therefore and see, that it is an evil thing and bitter, that you have forsaken the Lord your God, and that my fear is not in you, says the Lord God of hosts' (Jer. 2:19). There is a twofold evil in sin, which the soul is now sensible of:

With respect to themselves, they are sensible of the bitter fruits of sin: 'What fruit had you then in those things, of which you are now ashamed? For the end of those things is death' (Rom. 6:21). They see now 'the vine is the vine of Sodom, the grapes are grapes of gall, the clusters bitter, and their teeth are set on edge.' They cry out, as the sons of the prophets in another case, 'O you man of God, there is death in the pot' (2 Kings 4:40). This is the danger of sin, that they are made sensible of. They see the guilt of it, laying the soul open to temporal, spiritual, and eternal strokes: 'O Lord, though our iniquities testify against us, do you it for your name's sake: for our backslidings are many, we have sinned against you' (Jer. 14:7). Hence, 'horror takes hold on them, because of God's righteous judgments.' They wonder that they are not in hell, drinking the cup of the wrath of God. Their hearts tremble to look back on the ruin that was hanging over their heads in their natural state; that the poisonous cup which they drank has not despatched them. Hence they fear to meddle with sin again, as one would do to take a serpent into his bosom.

With respect to God and Christ, in a threefold respect:

1. As contrary to the holy law of God: 'Whosoever commits sin transgresses also the law: for sin is the transgression of the law' (1 John 3:4). By sin one breaks over the hedge, yea, breaks it down, and so steps into the devil's ground; what wonder then a serpent do bite him! Now the sinner sees the equity of God's law, and so plainly perceives the evil of transgression: 'The law is holy; and the commandment holy, and just, and good' (Rom. 7:12). And the breaking over this so glorious a hedge, galls the penitent heart, the ingenuous spirit of an evangelical penitent.

2. As contrary to the holy nature of God: 'You are of purer eyes than to behold evil, and cannot look on iniquity' (Hab. 1:13). Sin is the worst of evils in itself, and in the eyes of the penitent. There is nothing so contrary to the chief good, and therefore it is the chief evil. Now, the true penitent loves God, his holy nature and perfections; and therefore his sin is heavy to him, because by it he has walked contrary to him: 'Woe to us that we have sinned' (Lam. 5:16).

3. As the procuring cause of the sufferings of Christ: 'They will look upon me whom they have pierced, and they

will mourn for him' (Zech. 12:10). Mount Calvary is the Bochim to the true penitent; the sufferings of Christ are the commentaries on sin, which the true penitent reads; the groans of a dying Saviour rend their hearts; and by the wounds of a Redeemer they see the ill of sin.

This is the loathsomeness of sin (Isa. 30:22); whereby it is not only hated for what attends it, but is abhorred for itself, as a thing which on no terms the soul could any longer digest.

The qualities of this sense of sin

A particular and distinct sense of sin, not a general and confused one. No man hears the gospel, having common understanding, but he confesses himself a sinner; but many nevertheless are blind as to particulars. But this puts one in a capacity to lay his hands on his sores, saying, 'Against you, you only have I sinned, and done this evil in your sight' (Ps. 51:4). It shows him his particular transgressions in which he has exceeded, and the particular ills by which he has exceeded and offended in these. As the vermin appear crawling, when the stone is lifted up, which before lay hid; so the ills of the heart and life appear to the penitent: 'I was alive without the law once: but when the commandment came, sin revived, and I died' (Rom. 7:9).

It is real, not imaginary. The Spirit of the Lord realises the evil of sin to the soul. And so it goes beyond a merely rational knowledge of sin, as far as the sense of the bitterness of gall got by tasting it, exceeds that got by the bare hearing of it: 'Your own wickedness will correct you, and your backslidings will reprove you: know therefore and see, that it is an evil thing and bitter, that you have forsaken the Lord your God, and that my fear is not in you, says the

Lord God of hosts' (Jer. 2:19). There is a spiritual sensation of spiritual things, arising from the new nature, as well as a natural feeling of what is grievous to us another way: 'The natural man receives not the things of the Spirit of God; for they are foolishness to him: neither can he know them, because they are spiritually discerned. But he that is spiritual judges all things' (1 Cor. 2:14-15).

It is operative, not dead and idle. The eye of the penitent affects his heart; and the heart being touched, sets all the powers of the soul to work. It is the spiritual physic, that ceases not to work till the whole soul be purged; as in the case of Peter's hearers, 'who were pricked in their heart, and said to Peter, and to the rest of the apostles, Men and brethren, what will we do?' (Acts 2:37). There is a sense of sin which vents itself in nothing but in sighing and going backward, or in dry and fruitless complaints. It is like the disturbance which the sluggard meets with on his bed, which never thoroughly awakens him. But his sense of sin is thorough work.

It is an abiding sense of sin, not a transient one in a fit, and so goes away, 'My eye trickles down, and ceases not, without any intermission; till the Lord look down, and behold from heaven' (Lam. 3:49-50). The humbled soul carries the body of sin and death about with him, saying with the apostle, 'O wretched man that I am! Who will deliver me from the body of this death?' (Rom. 7:24). For it is not a slight touch, which goes as it comes, very easily. The removal of the stroke carries off Pharaoh's sense of sin; but here the wound is deeper and so more abiding.

Using the Truth

> An insensible sinner is an unhumbled impenitent sinner; as was the case of the church of Laodicea, who said, 'she was rich, and increased with goods, and had need of nothing; and did not know that she was wretched, and miserable, and poor, and blind, and naked (Rev. 3:17). They that never digged deep, are not built on the rock. They that have never got a broad sight of themselves in the sinfulness of their hearts and lives, have never yet got a believing sight of Christ. Consider this, you that have still lived at ease, strangers to any thorough exercise about your soul's case; though the door is shut, the thief is in the house.

> This shows how it comes that the pride of people's hearts still remains, though under crying guilt of sin. Though they know their sin, they have no due sense of it. If they had, it would be such a burden on their backs as would soon make them stoop, as Peter's hearers did (Acts 2:37). Insensible sinners may sit high in the seat of the scornful, while they see not what a God they have to do with: but when the Spirit of the Lord opens their eyes, and touches their hearts, to let them see and feel the evil of sin, they will lie low in the dust. They will 'put their mouth in the dust, if so be there may be hope' (Lam. 3:29).

> See here a difference between the saint's humiliation, and that of the hypocrite's. An Ahab may humble himself from a sense of the danger of sin; but a true penitent is humbled from the sense of the loathsomeness of sin (1 Kings 21:27-9; Job 42:5-6). A slave may bow himself for fear of the whip; but the disposition of a son is to be affected with the offence done to a kind father. Many will seem very low under the rod of God, and the apprehensions of this wrath, who are never touched with his love. They will be cast down under the sense of the evil their sin does to themselves, while the dishonour done to God by it lies far from their hearts.

> Let me exhort you to get and entertain a deep sense of sin on your spirits. See your sins, and be duly affected with them, and be humbled for them. O how sad is it, that amongst our many thoughts, sin gets so few of them! For motives to press this exhortation, consider:

>> That the Lord is anew calling the land by his providence to be sensible of their sins, and to be humbled for them. The Lord took it not long ago as a brand out of the burning; but he is threatening to cast it into the fire again, by a foreign invasion. For though we were delivered, yet the controversy remains still. We have not been thankful for our deliverance; atheism, profanity, formality, contempt of the gospel, and a spirit of apostacy and declining from the Lord, and his work and way, woefully abound. How can we miss to fall at length!

>> The present dispensation of providence towards this congregation, threatening to leave our house desolate. It fills the mouths of many with what is little worth; would to God it might fill your hearts and mine with a serious inquiry into the causes of it before the Lord. It speaks aloud, O that we were taking up the language of the threatening rod. The melancholy state of this congregation, in the time of the last desolation, needs not be forgot. It would become us all very well on this occasion, to consider what a jealous God we have to do with, and what entertainment has been given to the preached gospel; to lay our hands everyone on our own mouths, and consider well what we have contributed to the bringing of the matter to this pass. By taking with our sin, and humbling ourselves before the Lord, way might be made for the acceptance of prayer through Jesus Christ; and them that humble themselves, God will exalt.

>> However lightly your sins may sit on your spirits, they are a burden to the holy Spirit of God: "'Behold,' says the Lord, 'I am pressed under you, as a cart is pressed that is full of sheaves'" (Amos 2:13). And we may be sure the Lord will ease himself of that burden sooner or later. And if it be not by our repentance and humiliation, it will be by his accomplishing his wrath on us: 'Ah, I will ease me of my adversaries, and avenge me of my enemies' (Isa. 1:24). Therefore consider your ways in order to return to the Lord. The lighter that sin sits on us, it is the more grieving to the Spirit of the Lord.

>> Without a sense of sin there is no humiliation; that without humiliation there can be no repentance; and that without repentance there can be no escape from the wrath of God. 'For unless you repent, you will perish.' Insensibleness of sin, and the evil of it, locks up the heart in obduration and impenitency; and that will shut up the soul under wrath. But God loves the sensible humbled son: 'Is Ephraim my dear son? Is he a pleasant child? For since I spoke against him, I do earnestly remember him still: therefore my bowels are troubled for him; I will surely have mercy upon him, says the Lord' (Jer. 31:20).

Sorrow

In true humiliation there is a kindly sorrow for sin:

> I will pour upon the house of David, and upon the inhabitants of Jerusalem, the spirit of grace and of supplications; and they will look upon me whom they have pierced, and they will mourn for him as one mourns for his only son, and will be in bitterness for him, as one that is in bitterness for his first-born. (Zech. 12:10)

The soul is not only filled with remorse, but true grief, for offending a holy, gracious God. He grieved the Spirit in committing sin, his spirit is grieved in repenting of it. The hard heart is broken, the adamantine heart dissolved into tears of godly sorrow, the rock is struck by the rod of the gospel, and the waters gush out. The way to Zion lies through the valley of Baca:

> 'In those days, and in that time,' says the Lord, 'the children of Israel will come, they and the children of Judah together, going and weeping: they will go, and seek the Lord their God. They will ask the way to Zion with their faces thitherward, saying, Come, and let us join ourselves to the Lord, in a perpetual covenant that will not be forgotten.' (Jer. 50:4-5)

And it is the mourners for sin whom the Lord comforts with the consolations of his Spirit. This is that brokenness and contrition of heart, which God calls for, and takes so much pleasure in. This is the rending of the heart, which God requires (Joel 2:12-13).

The properties of godly sorrow

It is *sorrow for sin as sin*; not only for the guilt of it, but the loathsomeness of it; not only for the ill it does to ourselves, but the dishonour and wrong it does to a holy gracious God (Ps. 51:4; Zech. 12:10). The penitent in his sorrow, goes farther than awakened reprobates, who seeing their souls ruined and dead, do put on their mournings. He grieves at the heart, because of the offence done to God, the defacing of his image, transgressing a holy and most just law, furnishing a spear and nails to pierce a Saviour.

It is *inward real sorrow*. Not the hanging down of the head like a bulrush (Isa. 58:5). Not a made sorrow in a disfigured countenance, which lies all in outward appearance. But it is a sorrow soaking into the soul, and piercing the very heart (Isa. 61:3), making him mourn before the Lord, when the world knows nothing of it. For it arises from an inward principle.

It is *lively sorrow*. The sorrow of the world works death. It stupifies a man, and takes heart and hand for duty from him. But the spiritual pangs of godly sorrow for sin quicken a man to his duty: 'For behold, this self-same thing that you sorrowed after a godly sort, what carefulness it wrought in you, yea, what clearing of yourselves, yea, what indignation, yea, what fear, yea, what vehement desire, yea, what zeal, yea, what revenge' (2 Cor. 7:11). It makes the man active in salvation-work. And the reason is, the one springs from slavish fear, which chills the soul, making it cold and stiff, and unfit for action; the other from love, which warms the heart, and disposes it for action: 'Her sins which are many, are forgiven: for she loved much' (Luke 7:47).

It is *abiding sorrow*. It is not a flash of affection, which is deceitful, but a 'spirit of heaviness' (Isa. 61:3). The sorrows of many are like a summer-shower, that wets the surface of the ground, but quickly dries up, before it does any good. But godly sorrow is like that, 'Sorrow is better than laughter: for by the sadness of the countenance the heart is made better' (Eccles. 7:3). The soul, like Mary, mourns till it find the Lord (Lam. 3: 49-50). It may indeed remit of its degrees; but while sin abides, the spring of mourning abides too.

It is *universal sorrow*. The true penitent heartily grieves for his own sin (Ps. 38:18), and for the sin of others (Ps. 119:136). It is like the letting out of waters: it may begin at one sin, but it does not stop there, but goes through all known sin (Ps. 1:5), and unknown too: 'Who can understand his errors? Cleanse you me from secret faults' (Ps. 19:12). They never truly mourn for one sin, that do not mourn for all: for that which moves sorrow in the repenting heart for one sin, is to be found in all sins, namely, its contrariety to the law and nature of God, the loathsomeness as well as danger of it. And hence, when once the floodgate of godly sorrow is opened, it overflows all; and the sweetest morsel becomes bitter.

It is *deep sorrow*. Peter repenting wept bitterly. He that would have a good crop, ploughs well; and he that would build surely, goes deep with the foundation. It was the want of depth of earth that was the ruin of the stony-ground hearers (Matt. 13:5). And deep digging was the safety of the house founded on a rock (Luke 6:48). This sorrow is a rending of the heart (Joel 2:13); a rending of it as the plough rends the earth (Jer. 4:3); a pricking and piercing of it as with daggers, swords, and spears (Acts 2:37, compared with John 19:34); a cutting it as with a knife (Jer. 4:4).

It is a question, whether penitential sorrow exceeds all other sorrows for the comforts of this life, or not? If we measure by the moving of the heart and affections, it is evident, that it does not always exceed other sorrows. But if we measure by the settled disposition of the heart, it is as evident that it exceeds them all. As the deepest waters ordinarily make least noise, so men will be more moved in a lesser joy and grief than in a greater; for they are but the lightest joys that move laughter, and often the greatest sorrows are above tears. It settles more firmly, and continues more than any other sorrow whatsoever in the world.

It is *heart purifying sorrow*. It works repentance or forsaking of sin: 'Godly sorrow works repentance to salvation, not to be repented of' (2 Cor. 7:10). True mourning and turning are inseparable companions; though there is a mourning for sin, that is not deep enough to turn up the love of sin by the root. True sorrow in the heart is a spring, which as it runs will work out sin, as to the love, habitual practice, and dominion of it, as a spring works out the mud thrown into it.

Using the Truth

> There is no repenting with a hale heart, and without repentance no
> salvation. People must either be broken for their sins in a way of
> mourning, or God will break them for them in a way of judgment.
> There are many stout hearts in our day, that will boldly outface
> challenges from the word and their own consciences, without either
> breaking or bowing. But let such remember, that there is a day coming
> when God will make the stoutest heart to tremble, and the heart of
> adamant to fly in a thousand pieces: 'You will break them with a rod
> of iron, you will dash them in pieces like a potter's vessel' (Ps. 2:9).

> How far must they be from humiliation, that sin deliberately,
> glory in their shame, and rejoice in ungodly courses and practices!
> I think providences and ordinances are hardening to many in
> our day; they are not bettered by them, and therefore they are
> hardened and made worse under them. Our penny weddings and
> set drinkings, leaving such a stench behind them, and attended
> with before unheard of profanity, are speaking evidences of this.
> Are these Christian methods to help poor people? Will God
> accept the gift, where such a fat sacrifice is offered to the devil?
> Is that charity for which drinking must open men's hearts and
> hands to give? If some methods be not fallen on to prevent these
> things, they will bring wrath on the congregation. I appeal to the
> consciences of all sober persons, if it looked not judgment-like,
> that in that very time when abroad a design was managing to
> lay the congregation desolate, at home many were met for a set
> drinking, carried on to a monstrous height of profanity, in the
> day and in the night. It becomes us all to mourn for this, lest we
> involve ourselves in the guilt. And particularly I warn all such
> as were any way partakers of that scandalous riot, to repent, lest
> wrath break out upon them. For it is a fearful thing to stand
> exposed to the lash of these threatenings: 'Woe to him that gives
> his neighbour drink: putting your bottle to him, and making
> him drunk, that you may look on their nakedness' (Hab. 2:15).

> 'And in that day did the Lord of hosts call to weeping, and to mourning, and to baldness, and to girding with sackcloth: and behold, joy and gladness, slaying oxen, and killing sheep, eating flesh, and drinking wine; let us eat and drink, for tomorrow we will die. And it was revealed in my ears by the Lord of hosts, surely this iniquity will not be purged from you, till you die, says the Lord God of hosts.' (Isa. 22:12-14)

> The sorrow of many for their sins, will tend to no good account before the Lord. Few have any remarkable sorrow for their sins at all; but amongst those whose hearts are really grieved and pained for their sin, how few are there that have any right sorrow? The danger of it, the disadvantage by it, the shame of it before the world, pains them a little; but the dishonour done to God by it touches them not effectually. And so their sorrow will be but the beginning of hell, not of repentance.

> Be exhorted to mourn for sin. Labour to get your hearts affected with this mournful object, and be not strangers to this exercise. The sins and threatened judgments of this day call for it; and it is the way to attain particular safety in common calamity: 'And the Lord said to him, Go through the midst of the city, through the midst of Jerusalem, and set a mark upon the foreheads of the men that sigh, and that cry for all the abominations that be done in the midst thereof' (Ezek. 9:4). If we were more in the duty of mourning, we would share more of the gospel-comforts: 'Blessed are they that mourn: for they will be comforted' (Matt. 5:4). And the more of the Spirit one has, the more will he be taken up that way.

Shame

In true humiliation there is a holy shame upon the account of sin before the Lord: 'What fruit had you in those things, of which you are now ashamed? For the end of those things is death' (Rom. 6:21) The remembrance of sin fills the penitent with shame and blushing: hence says Ezra, 'O my God, I am ashamed and blush to lift up my face to you, my God: for our iniquities are increased over our head, and our trespass is grown up to the heavens' (ch. 9:6). Shame was never known in the world, till sin entered; yet sometimes sin comes to such a height with sinners, that it quite banishes shame: but the case of such is very desperate, 'You had a whore's forehead; you refused to be ashamed' (Jer. 3:3). Shame then is the remains of virtue in a sinner, to which whoever are lost, all are lost to all good: 'The show of their countenance witnesses against them, and they declare their sin as Sodom, they hide it not' (Isa. 3:9). Now, the grace of God awakens this shame, and sanctifies it in the penitent soul, so that he hangs down his head before the Lord, as ashamed of his way and heart.

Four causes of shame

Nakedness. Hence said Adam to the Lord, 'I heard your voice in the garden: and I was afraid, because I was naked; and I hid myself' (Gen. 3:10). Sin strips the sinners of their beautiful garments, takes away the glory of the rational creature, and leaves them without a covering before the eyes of a holy God. The penitent sees this, and is ashamed; and so the publican, cannot lift up his eyes to heaven, but smites on his breast, as if he would wound the breast that sin bred in, which has brought him to this shameful case.

Pollution and defilement, for that makes one loathsome to others: 'You will plunge me in the ditch, and my own clothes will abhor me' (Job 9:31). Sin defiles the soul, takes away and mars all its beauty, and deforms it in the sight of God. And the penitent sees this, and is ashamed, 'We are all as an unclean thing, and all our righteousnesses are as filthy rags, and we all do fade as a leaf, and our iniquities, like the wind, have taken us away' (Isa. 64:6). Never was a man that had been plunged over head and ears in a mire, more ashamed to come before others in that case, than the penitent is ashamed to show his face before God.

Disappointment of raised expectations (Jer. 2:36-7). The sinner in his impenitent state, looked for his happiness and satisfaction in sinful courses. But when his heart is touched, he is ashamed; for he finds, that instead of bread expected, he has got a stone, instead of fish, a serpent. He finds, that he has been courting his death and ruin; and that from the wall he leaned on, there has come forth a serpent and bit him. And hence is that reflection, 'What fruit had you in those things, of which you are now ashamed? For the end of those things is death' (Rom. 6:21).

Discovering of one's reproach. 'Sin is a reproach to any people' (Prov. 14:34). In the impenitent state, the soul's reproach is hid to it; but when grace touches the heart, and the Lord brings the sinner's ways to mind, lays his sins in broad-band before him, how can he miss to be ashamed? In a special manner, a conviction of base ingratitude fills one with shame, as to be convicted of designs against him who had saved our life. And thus the goodness of God duly considered, fills the penitent with shame and blushing, while he thinks what an ungrateful wretch he has been: 'We lie down in our shame, and our confusion covers us: for we have sinned against the Lord our God, we and our fathers from our youth even to this day, and have not obeyed the voice of the Lord our God' (Jer. 3:25).

Using the Truth

> Shamelessness in sin is a badge of impenitency, and therefore a forerunner of destruction (Jer. 6:15; Phil. 3:19). A forehead of brass is a sign the heart is of stone. Impudence in sin argues a filthy heart, an obstinate disposition, and a seared conscience. And such are a stage beyond others from the kingdom of God. What hopes can they have of the glory of heaven, that glory in their shame?

> We see, then, that sin will bring shame sooner or later, here or hereafter. As for them that live and die without repentance, their shame is sure, and they will be covered with it, before the great congregation of heaven and earth at the last day, and they will never recover their countenance: 'Many of them that sleep in the dust of the earth will awake, some to shame and everlasting contempt'(Dan. 12:2). And if people be recovered by repentance, they will be filled with shame before the Lord, even holy shame. But whatever shame men have, it is no holy shame that keeps them from glorifying God by taking shame to themselves when called to do so; for no grace of God keeps folk back from duty (Josh. 7:19). Common discretion teaches, that one ashamed of an injury done to the honour of another, cannot look him in the face but with shame, till he has done what he can to repair that honour.

> The penitent soul is an ingenuous soul, and heartily at odds with sin. For such an one will be ashamed before God, of what the world cannot tax him with. Many may be sorry for sin before God, because of the terrible consequences of it which they apprehend, who yet are not ashamed before him, because they see not the evil that is in itself. But it argues a childlike disposition, to be heartily ashamed of secret sins before the Lord.

Self-Loathing

In true humiliation there is self-loathing and abhorrence: 'Then will you remember your own evil ways, and your doings that were not good, and will loathe yourselves in your own sight, for your iniquities, and for your abominations' (Ezek. 36:31). The penitent not only loathes his sin, but himself for his sin. He cries out with Job, 'Behold I am vile, what will I answer you? I will lay my hand upon my mouth' (Job 40:4). Repentance sets a man at variance with himself. He sees his ugly face in the glass of God's law, Christ sufferings, and the Lord's goodness, and he loathes himself.

How self-loathing manifests itself in the penitent

The penitent justly entertains *low and mean thoughts of himself.* True penitents see such vileness in themselves, as makes them give a very mean account of themselves. Abraham owned himself to be dust and ashes; Jacob, less than all the mercies of God; David, a worm, and not a man; Asaph, as a beast before the Lord; Agur, more brutish than any; the centurion, unworthy that Christ should come under his roof; Paul, one born out of due time, the least of the apostles, no, less than the least of all saints, no the chief of sinners; and the prodigal son (Luke 15:19), reckoned himself no more worthy to be called a son, but to be made a hired servant.

He is heartily *out with himself* upon the account of his sin: 'Wherefore I abhor myself, and repent in dust and ashes' (Job 42:6). As one cannot with any pleasure touch himself, that has filth thrown on him, but his very heart stands at himself; so it is in spiritual self-loathing. He looks on himself as an ugly spectacle. He not only has nothing to say in defence of himself, but with indignation he rejects all the shifts and excuses for it, which he was satisfied with before: 'The publican standing afar off, would not lift up so much as his eyes to heaven, but smote upon his breast, saying, "God be merciful to me a sinner"' (Luke 18:13).

In *holy revenge* (2 Cor. 7:11). He that was going on in sin before, is now divided against himself; so that the devil's kingdom of sin in him must needs go to ruin. He acts the part of an accuser, advocate, and judge, against himself; yea in some sort lashes himself for his sinful heart and life. Hence we find the humbled sinner:

1. Smiting on his breast (Luke 18:13), as if declaring, that he deserves to be struck at the heart, and die for his transgression; that within him is the cause of all his sin and sorrows, he may thank himself for all; the source and spring of all is the corrupt heart.

2. Smiting on his thigh (Jer. 31:19), as if he would thereby declare, that he would be willing to take vengeance on the feet that carried him out of the way of God; that he is filled with indignation against himself, for his unaccountable practices, saying, What have I done? What a wretched sinner have I been?

What arouses self-loathing in the penitent?

The remarkable *blots, and signal miscarriages* in his way, that deeply wound and defile the conscience: like Peter's denying his Master, which made him weep bitterly, when he came to himself. These in a peculiar manner cover the soul with confusion, and fill it with self-abhorrence. Sometimes repentance begins at some such thing, from whence it spreads to the whole body of sin: 'Let all the house of Israel know assuredly, that God has made that same Jesus whom you have crucified, both Lord and Christ. Now when they heard this, they were pricked in their heart, and said, "Men and brethren, what will we do?"' (Acts 2:36-7).

The *fullness of sin seen in the soul*: 'We are all as an un-clean thing, and all our righteousnesses are as filthy rags' (Isa. 64:6). The penitent being made sensible of his soul's case, sees the leprosy spread over the whole man, his mind under much darkness, his will rebellious against the will of God, his affections disordered, his whole nature cor-rupted, the seed of every sin in it; so that he concludes, that his heart is full of iniquity, and that the lusts that are hatched there, their name may be Legion. His life is a loathsome spectacle of the outbreakings and working of that corruption. So that he sees that 'from the sole of the foot to the crown of the head there is no soundness; and therefore he loathes himself.'

The *pollution cleaving to his duties*. While he sees how the running sore of his natural corruption drops on all his holy things, and defiles them, how can he choose but loathe himself? He sees his best works are like a moth-eaten gar-ment, full of holes; never a prayer, nor confession made, but there are provocations against the Lord in them. His mournings for sin must be mourned over, because of the woeful defects thereof; while he goes to mend one hole, still he is sure to strike out another. Thus the penitent is in his own eyes like Job, who had not whole fingers to dress his sores with; so he abhors himself.

The *aggravations of sin* (Luke 15:18). A sight of these makes sin look like an opened stinking sore, in which each of them contributes to make it more and more loathsome. When the penitent considers with what bent of affection he has sinned, the light, the many mercies, vows, and resolu-tions, he has sinned against, he cannot but loathe himself as a wretched self-destroyer, as an ungrateful miscreant, and as a beast before the Lord.

Instability in any thing that is good: 'Your goodness is as a morning cloud, and as the early dew it goes away' (Hosea 6: 4). Wavering hearts, and wavering hands, are very humbling to a soul truly touched. A good frame is a rare hour, and stays but a short while. How often are resolutions fairly taken up, and begin to bud in endeavours for practice, that yet are quickly let fall again? How often do men relapse into the same sins they have sometimes had made very bitter to them? Nothing is more apt than this to stir up self-abhorrence.

Using the Truth

> Self-conceit is a need-nail to a state of impenitency: 'You say, I am rich, and increased with goods, and have need of nothing; and do not know that you are wretched, and miserable, and poor, and blind, and naked.' No repentance can be where there is no humiliation, and there can be no humiliation while people are puffed up with a conceit of themselves. Publicans and harlots will enter into the kingdom of heaven, before such self-conceited professors. Whenever the Spirit of the Lord takes a dealing with such persons, and discovers to them the signal miscarriages in their life, the fullness of sin, that swelling conceit of sweet self will fall away, as ever the snow melts in a sunshine day. They that look on themselves as among the chief of saints, will see themselves the chief of sinners.

> Look into yourselves, if you would loathe yourselves and repent. Hence said Isaiah, 'Woe is me, for I am undone, because I am a man of unclean lips' (Isa. 6:5). Things may be going all wrong in the house, and the master not know it, while he is a stranger at home. Many a poor soul is pining away in its iniquity, and running with loathsome spiritual sores, threatening its ruin, while in the meantime they are mightily in love with themselves, and fond of their own condition, like a miserable man that is happy in a dream. But heavy will the awakening of such be.

> Sin must needs be a very loathsome thing in the eyes of a peni-
> tent, since it makes him loathe himself. Alas! Many times we
> love that in ourselves, which we loathe in others. But when one
> loathes himself for his sin against a holy, gracious God, it is an
> argument that that soul is heartily out with sin.

Confession

In true humiliation there is a penitent confession of sin.
Hence is that exhortation, 'Only acknowledge your iniquity, that you have transgressed against the Lord your
God' (Jer. 3:13). This is the way that penitent sinners have
always sought pardon and ease to their consciences in:
'I acknowledged my sin to you, and my iniquity have I not
hid: I said, I will confess my transgressions to the Lord;
and you forgave the iniquity of my sin' (Ps. 32:5). Confession of sin is the vomit of sin, whereby the sweet morsel
is cast up again; and it is the vent of real sorrow, shame,
and self-abhorrence. And when the heart is loosed to it,
the man becomes like the fish that is boiled in the water
which it swam in.

This confession is to be according to the nature of the
offence. If the sin be secret one, a confession to God in
secret is sufficient. 'Confess your faults one to another.' If
it be a public offence, giving public scandal, the confession
is to be public also: 'Them that sin rebuke before all, that
others also may fear' (1 Tim. 5:20). So penitent David left
his confession on record, for the church's edification. And
so did the apostle Paul (1 Tim. 1:13). And the reason is
evident, since by sin God's honour is impaired, and we
can repair it no other way, but by confessing it with sorrow and shame. The confession must be according to the

nature of the offence, else the wrong done to the honour of God is not repaired by it. And in the private and public confession God is our party, and not men only, as well as in the secret one.

Now, confession is a necessary part of humiliation. If the hard heart be loosed to be truly humbled for sin, it follows course, that the tongue will be loosed to confess it. Hence, confession is put for the whole of humiliation, yea of repentance, 'I will go and return to my place, till they acknowledge their offence' (Hosea 5:15). 'If we confess our sins, he is faithful, and just to forgive our sins, and to cleanse us from all unrighteousness' (1 John 1:9).

Confession of sin has two parts
Self-accusing. God has given a law, the sinner has broken it; the penitent confesses his transgression with shame and sorrow, to the honour of the lawgiver. He cannot hide it, he dares not deny it; his soul is humbled, and therefore he confesses it: 'I acknowledge my transgressions: and my sin is ever before me' (Ps. 51:3). He approves of the law as holy, just, and good, and disapproves of the transgression. Thus the morsel that was sweet in the mouth, turning bitter in the belly, is vomited up.

Self-condemning. Hence said the returning prodigal: 'Father, I have sinned against heaven, and before you, and am no more worthy to be called your son' (Luke 15:18-19). The penitent looks to the law, and the demerit of his sin, reads his own doom, and passes sentence on himself. He owns that all the evil he smarts under for the present, is just and righteous with God: 'Therefore has the Lord watched upon the evil, and brought it upon us: for the Lord our God is righteous in all his works which he does: for we have not obeyed his voice' (Dan. 9:14). If his broken bones pain him, he will own that it is just. If his sin find him, so that he read it in his punishment, he will acknowledge that it is a just contrivance; and that he deserves to sink under eternal wrath for it, saying with the afflicted church, 'It is of the Lord's mercies that we are not consumed, because his compassions fail not' (Lam. 3:22). He will say, that God may justly take the filthy garments of his sin, cover them with brimstone, wrap him up in them, and cast him into the pit (Ps. 51:4).

Now, this confession should be sincere, full, very particular, free, and accompanied with forsaking.

Using the Truth

> Hiding and covering sin, and refusing to confess it in the way that God calls for a confession, is a sign of an heart not humbled for it: 'He that covers his sins will not prosper: but whoever confesses and forsakes them, will have mercy' (Prov. 28:13). Many, falling into public scandals by their works of darkness, put on a forehead of brass, and refuse to confess them for the glory of God, cheating themselves that they will confess their sins to God but not to men. Little do they consider, that by that means they put a bar in their own way to pardon, while by resolute lying they cover one sin with another, and by refusing to honour God at his call. Nor do they consider the weight of that word standing in the way of their peace with God, while they refuse to remove the scandal, so that they may be reconciled to the church: 'If he will neglect to hear them, tell it to the church: but if he neglect to hear the church, let him be to you as an heathen man, and a publican. Verily I say to you, Whatever you will bind on earth, will be bound in heaven: and whatsoever you will loose on earth, will be loosed in heaven' (Matt. 18:17-18). It is true, it is but a word; yea but it is God's word, that will be more terrible to an awakened conscience than any punishment men can inflict.

> They that shun to see their sins, that they may confess them, cannot repent of them: 'Your habitation is in the midst of deceit, through deceit they refuse to know me, says the Lord. Therefore thus says the Lord of hosts, behold I will melt them, and try them; for how will I do for the daughter of my people?' (Jer. 9:6-7). It is true, there are sins which we cannot so see in ourselves as to confess them particularly; but in that case the soul does not refuse conviction: 'Who can understand his errors? Cleanse me from secret faults' (Ps. 19:12). But when one keeps the sweet morsel under his tongue, and has no will to see the evil of it, lest he should be obliged to confess it before the Lord, this is another case, and speaks a deceit of the heart, holding fast sin, and refusing to let it go.

> Labour to be sincere, full, free, in confessing your sins. We are in debt to the justice of God, we cannot pay our debt; let us confess our debt, to prevent a pursuit, and that we may be capable to pray for forgiveness of it, which otherwise we cannot be. O, if we had a due sense and sorrow for our sins, this would, like an overflowing flood, bear down before them all those things which now hamper us in confessing our sins.

Turning to God from Sin

I come now to the second thing, namely the returning of the soul to God from sin. This is the completing of repentance. Whatever sense of sin, shame, and sorrow, one have for it, if it end not in returning to God, it is naught. It is under this notion that repentance is so often called for in the Old Testament: Return, Turn. And it may be well put for the whole of repentance for:

1. The impenitent sinner is out of himself, out of his wits; but by repentance he returns and comes to himself. Hence we read, that the prodigal came to himself (Luke 15:17). There is never a soul that is brought to repentance, but

there is as great a change upon him, as on a madman that is returned to his sound mind. He has quite other notions of things than he had before; he looks upon his sinful courses as the effects of spiritual frenzy. This is the first part of repentance, namely, humiliation.

2. The impenitent sinner is out of his place, like a wandering bird: 'As a bird that wanders from her nest: so is a man that wanders from his place' (Prov. 27:8). And so the soul is out of its rest, and out of its duty. Adam shook himself and all his race out of their rest, and out of that they wander up and down in the devil's common. Repentance is the sinner's returning to his place again, to take up his place again in God's house among his servants. This is the second part of repentance. And whenever the soul comes to itself, it will come to God again. The grace of God finds the sinner, as the angel found Hagar (Gen. 16:8-9); and as Paul found Onesimus (Philem. 10-12).

Turning from Sin

There is a turning from sin: 'Repent, and turn from your idols, and turn away your faces from all your abominations' (Ezek. 14:6). 'Let every one that names the name of Christ, depart from iniquity' (2 Tim. 2:19). 'Depart from evil' (Ps. 34:14). The sinner changes his course, and gives up with his former lusts. The impenitent sinner is a misled traveller, who finding himself wrong, will go no farther on, but leave the wrong way, and seek the right one. To repent of sin, and yet continue in the practice of it, is a contradiction. No; the true penitent ceases from sin, he gives over his work in the service of sin and lusts (Isa. 1:16). He forsakes his former ways (Isa. 55:7). And though sin remains in him, yet it reigns not as before.

Longing to drop the chains

True penitents turn from sin in their heart and affection. There is a bond in the impenitent state, whereby the sinner's heart is knit to his lusts, as ever the sucking child's heart is to the breast, which he can by no means want. Repentance looses that bond: 'O wretched man that I am! Who will deliver me from the body of this death?' (Rom. 7:24). So, though sins cleaves to the soul, yet the soul cleaves not to it as formerly. It hangs on him, it is true, but only as the chains on the captive, which are his burden; as the grave-clothes on Lazarus raised, which he is working to put off. Thus repentance makes a change of the heart.

His esteem of sin is turned to despite. His judgment is set against it: 'In that day a man will cast his idols of silver, and his idols of gold, which they made, each one for himself to worship, to the moles and to the bats' (Isa. 2:20). What he approved before, now he condemns; for the scales are turned, and what was highest before is now lowest. Grace and holiness get the ascendant of sin and wickedness in his esteem. Those he counted most happy sometimes, because they took the greatest liberty in sinful courses, he now accounts most miserable, as slaves to sin, and in the road to destruction; and therefore takes up Joshua's resolution, 'As for me and my house, we will serve the Lord' (Josh. 24:15).

His love of sin is turned to hatred (Ezek. 14:6). 'I hate vain thoughts' (Ps. 119:113). 'I hate every false way' (Ps. 119:128). It was good in his eyes before, better than the favour of God, and communion with him. He knew nothing good or desirable but the world and lusts, and what might satisfy the corrupt cravings of the soul. But repentance turns his soul against it, and he hates it as an evil thing, as the worst of evils, without fear of punishment, he would never choose it; for he hates it for itself, its contrariety to God's nature and will.

His liking of sin is turned to loathing. Hence repentance is called a casting away of sin (Ezek. 18:31), as one would do with some filthy thing that he cannot endure to have near him. For the penitent looks not only on sin as an ill thing, but as a loathsome thing which his heart stands at (Isa. 30:22). And this is the ground of that self-loathing which the penitent is filled with.

His cleaving to sin is turned into a longing to be rid of it (Rom. 7:24). The man longs to be free from it, as ever the prisoner for the opening of his prison-doors, the captive for his being set at liberty, and the dropping off of his chains. It is a burden on his back, which he groans under; a sickness to his soul, that he would fain have the cure of. And therefore Christ with all his salvation is lovely in his eyes; his sanctifying Spirit, as well as his justifying blood.

A visible change

They turn from it in their life and conversation. He that stood in the way of sinners before, now leaves it, when once the grace touches the heart (Isa. 55:7). The penitent not only has a pure heart, but clean hands. Repentance will make a visible change on one's life: for it sets men to mortify the members of the body of death (Rom. 8:13); to refuse compliance with lusts and temptations (Titus 2:12); to starve the lusts of the flesh (Rom. 13:14); and to nail the body of sin with all its members to the cross of Christ (Gal. 5:24).

They turn from the gross pollutions of the outward man (Ps. 24:3-4). An elect soul before conversion may be a habitual profane person, as well as others: but if he may be so after conversion, where is the difference between Christ's sheep and the devil's goats? It is true, they may make gross slips, as David and Peter did: but they do not lie in them, they recover again by repentance. A profane life is the mark of an impenitent state (Gal. 5:21). It is a wonder how men can pretend to repentance, while they live in the habitual practice of drunkenness, swearing, sabbath-breaking, lying, dishonesty, and other gross pollutions of the outward man, where one would think the profane devil is not so much as gone out, far less cast out.

They become tender with respect to the sins of common infirmity, labouring to make conscience of their words and actions (Acts. 24:16). What others account light of, they will stand at a distance from, as having felt the smart of sin; and that not only before the world, but even in secret where no eye sees but God's. They will stand aloof from temptations, and even from the appearance of evil: and in which they are overtaken through the frailty of the flesh, they will mourn for it before the Lord.

A fight to the death

In respect both of heart and life. They turn against sin to oppose and resist it, in the inner and outward man, as taking now the contrary side to the devil, the world, and the flesh. The spiritual combat is begun in the true penitent (Gal. 5:17). The war with sin is proclaimed and begun, which never ends till death. They revolt from, cast off the yoke, and stand up against their old masters (2 Tim. 2:19).

They resist the motions of sin in their hearts, and endeavour after heart purity, as well as life purity: 'I hate vain thoughts: but your law do I love' (Ps. 119:113). The Pharisaical professor may cleanse the outside of the platter, while he is little troubled about its being within full of ravening. But the hardest work a gracious soul has against sin, is with the heart, with what the world neither sees nor can see in him. And the guiding of the heart is the hardest piece of management in his religion.

They resist the outbreakings of sin in the life: 'I was also upright before him: and I kept myself from my iniquity' (Ps. 18:23). They see they are in a world where snares are thick laid; they see their own weakness, and how ready they are to be entrapped, and therefore labour to be on their guard, lest they be carried away with the stream. Hence they are afraid of temptations, and therefore labour to shut their eyes from beholding vanity; sometimes fearing to fall one day by the hand of temptation, and therefore longing to be beyond the reach of sin.

More than a day's work

Because their turning from sin is never perfect till death, therefore so long they are ay turning, and renewing their repentance. They are not true penitents who look on it as the work of some days or weeks, at the soul's first conversion to God (John 13:10). A true penitent will ay be repenting, as long as he is sinning. He sees that he is often falling into the mire, and therefore he must be often washing; daily contracting new debt, therefore must be daily crying for forgiveness. And the more heinous his after miscarriages be, the longer he lies secure, his repentance will be the more bitter when he rises up again.

Now, this turning from sin has these properties.

It is *voluntary*, as springing from an inward principle set up in the heart against sin: 'I abhor myself, and repent in dust and ashes' (Job 42:6). The penitent does not only cast away sin as a live coal out of his bosom, that would burn him, but as some loathsome thing, that would defile him. Some turn from their sins against their will; they part with their sin as Phaltiel did with his unlawful wife Michal (2 Sam. 3:15). They dwell in the tents of sin, till the rigging-tree break, and there is no abiding longer there for them; they part with their sins, as the covetous man with his riches at death, when, nill he will be, he must let it go. But true repentance is a turning from sin out of choice: and forced reformation neither is sincere nor will last (Ps. 78:34).

It is *sincere*, as being a turning from sin as sin, a turning from it because it is a turning away from God, a turning from it for its contrariety to God's holy nature and law (Luke 15:18). The man leaves his sin, not for the inferior motives only of danger to himself by it, but from the higher motives, namely, because it is offensive to God, dishonours his Son, grieves his Spirit, transgresses his law, and defaces his image. If your turning from sin proceeds not from these motives, God will never regard it as acceptable in his sight. It is done for self not for God; and God will never be the reward of that work of which he is not the end.

What should one do with respect to those sins he has turned from, from those lower motives of self, or those sins that have left him, before he left them? Do not turn back to them; but do with them as they used to do with those that die by their own hands, bury them disgracefully, and throw stones on their grave. Look on them and loathe them, rise higher in your motives to forsake them than before. You left them for your own sake, put them further away for the sake of God's honour. Set them before your eyes again, and see how provoking they have been to a holy God, how dishonouring to his Son. Repent and mourn over them on these accounts. And then your turning from them will be sincere.

This turning from sin is *universal*: 'I hate every false way' (Ps. 119:104). 'Cast away from you all your transgressions' (Ezek. 18:31). Whoever turns sincerely from one sin, turns from all known sin whatsoever; because the reason that moves the true penitent, is to be found in all as well as any one. Partial reformation is not sincere; for God requires the whole heart, and will not be served by halves. Every sin is a deadly wound to the soul; and therefore though many be cured, if but one remain uncured, the man is a dead man by that one: 'If your right eye offend you, pluck it out, and cast it from you: for it is profitable for you that one of your members should perish, and not that your whole body should be cast into hell' (Matt. 5:29). A drop of poison will make a whole cup of good wine deadly, and one sin retained will render all other reformation naught; as Abimelech the son of Jerubbaal's concubine was the death of all his seventy sons by his wives except one.

It is *speedy*, without delays: 'I made haste, and delayed not to keep your commandments' (Ps. 119:60). As long as a man is undetermined to turn from his sin, or delays to do it, his repentance is not sincere. It is an evidence that the lance of humiliation has not gone deep enough, when the filthy matter does not presently spring forth. A man whose heart is truly touched with a penitent sense of sin, will delay as long as the flinging a burning coal out of his bosom, as the casting away of his sin. No: when it goes to the quick, it must off presently; though it were an offending right hand, it must be cut off presently; though it were an offending right eye, it must be presently plucked out.

Not half-baked

This turning from sin is thorough; it makes complete work evangelically, though not legally. It was a flaw in Judah's repentance, that she turned not to the Lord with her whole heart, but feignedly (Jer. 3:10); and in Ephraim's that he mixed himself among the people, and was a cake not turned (Hosea 7:8). Men turn thoroughly from sin in these four respects.

The true penitent sticks at no known sin, but turns from all without exception, even those sins that are dearest and nearest to them, and which they have been most easily beset with (Heb. 12:1), 'I kept myself from my iniquity' (Ps. 18:23). This turning from sin is never thorough, till it reach the sin that is the sin of one's constitution, the sin that is the sin which most attends his calling, stations, and relations in which he stands; the sin that he has most frequent and strongest temptations to. That is the predominant evil which the heart must be loosed from, the right hand and right eye sin, the one thing lacking, which mars all other things (Mark 10:21). Unless there be a turning from, a warring with this, it is all wrong; though indeed they may sometimes lose as well as win in the battle.

He turns from that which is the ensnaring hook in any of his sins, the handle whereby it caught hold of him (Ps. 131:2). Pharaoh would have been content to let Israel go, so be they would have left their little ones, which he was sure would have brought them back again. And Satan will let people turn from sin for a time, while they retain a reigning love to the bewitching thing that is in a sinful course. For while it is so, the tree is indeed cut, but the root is left in the ground, and will grow again.

He turns from the occasions of sin (Ezek. 14:6). Wherefore David prays, 'Turn away my eyes from beholding vanity;' and Solomon gives advice in one case of drunkenness, 'Look not you upon the wine when it is red, when it gives his colour in the cup, when it moves itself aright' (Prov. 23:31). It is vain to pretend to repent and turn from sin, while men do not watch against the occasions of it, and wrestle against them, as against the sin itself. They that in a siege mind really do defend the town, they will defend the outworks as long as they can; wilfully to let the enemy in there, speaks treachery. Much lies in this point for reformation: 'Enter not into the path of the wicked, and go not in the way of evil men. Avoid it, pass not by it, turn from it, and pass away' (Prov. 4:14-15).

He turns from the enjoyment of the fruits of his sin. To pretend to turn from sin, and yet to feed sweetly on the fruits of it, is an absolutely vain pretence. When sin itself is truly quit, the profit of it is given up with. This the prophet teaches, 'He that walks righteously, and speaks uprightly, he that despises the gain of oppressions, that shakes his hands from holding of bribes, that stops his ears from hearing of blood, and shuts his eyes from seeing evil' (Isa. 33:15). This is so evident, that even Judas in his repentance, such as it was, could no longer brook the reward of his iniquity (Matt. 27:3). A philosopher had bought a pair of shoes, but had not paid the price of them; the tradesman died; the philosopher thought the money was gained; but his conscience caused him bring back the money, and throw it into the shop. 'Take it,' says he, 'you are alive to me, while dead to all the world besides.' Hence two things belong to this part of repentance:

1. Restitution, or restoring the thing again, which has been sinfully and wrongfully taken away from others. He that can do it, and will not, cannot repent of that sin; for he wilfully feeds on the fruit of his sin; and that is

a continuing in it inconsistent with turning from it. And since there is no pardon of that sin which a man does not repent of, it is a maxim in divinity, *Non remittitur nisi restituitur*, namely, to a person that is able, but unwilling to do it. Hence Zacchaeus proves himself a true penitent by restitution (Luke 19:8). And one may as well think a thief may repent in the time he is feeding on what he has stolen from his neighbour, as that one may repent of what in other cases he has unjustly taken from his neighbour, and can, but will not restore. When lovers part, they give back their tokens; and so when a sinner parts with his sin, he restores all that he had unjustly taken from others.

2. Reparation as far as may be, in those cases in which proper restitution cannot be made: as in the case of unjust wounding our neighbour's honour, reputation, peace, quiet, and contentment. Hence is that exhortation, 'Confess your faults one to another, and pray one for another, that you may be healed' (James 5:16). One may as well pretend to repent and go on in sin, as wilfully to refuse this and repent of the sin. The like reparation is necessary in those scandalous sins, whereby the honour of God is impaired before the world, religion wounded, and exposed to the contempt and scorn of profane men, and the hearts of the godly saddened. To repent of such sins, and yet wilfully to refuse the way whereby the honour of God, and the credit of religion, might in some measure be repaired is impossible. One may as well pretend to repent of his wounding a man, while he stands looking on him bleeding to death, and will not, though it is in his power, bind up his wounds.

Using the Truth

> Hence we may see what is the proper way to follow out the design of our congregational fast; namely, to turn from our sins which have provoked the Lord to wrath against us. For humiliation without reformation can do little service. Let each of us lay our hands to our hearts, and consider what has been the coal that we have cast in to raise this flame, and heartily turn from these things. If so, we would readily wear with thankfulness the blessings obtained by prayers.

> All the trouble, grief, and sorrow that men have for their sin is of little worth, if it issue not in turning from sin. For men to be sighing, but still going backward, is not repentance, but of that sort which may be carried on in hell, through eternity. If turning be not joined to mourning for sin, it is unsanctified sorrow, that will neither be acceptable to God, nor profitable to our souls.

> Turning from sin outwardly, while the heart remains glued to it, is not repentance either. It is an easy thing to reform outwardly; but the great business lies in getting the heart weaned from the world and lusts. If we would be satisfied as to the truth of our repentance, we must likewise examine the motives prevailing with us to turn from sin; for the mean and low motives that rise no higher than ourselves, our own advantage, ease, safety, will never denominate us true penitents.

> Repentance is not the work of a day or a year, but the work of our whole lives. For so turning from sin is. Sin follows us, while we flee from it; often does it overtake us, and so we must renew our flight. The whole life of a Christian is war; in that war are many battles, sometimes the Christian gains the day, and sometimes he loses. If he lose, he must renew the battle; if he win, he must pursue the victory, and lay his account with a new engagement. The great comfort is, that though he may lose a battle, yet he will be victorious in the war: 'The God of peace will bruise Satan under your feet shortly' (Rom. 16:20).

> See the necessity of turning from sin: 'Unless you repent,' says the text, 'you will all likewise perish.' Now, if you do not turn from sin, you do not repent; therefore if you turn not from it by repentance, you will perish. Our sins or our souls must go. Turn, or burn in the fire of God's wrath, is the choice. Let us then return speedily and thoroughly from all our iniquities, so will they not be our ruin.

Turning to God

In repentance there is a returning to God: 'Come, and let us return to the Lord' (Hosea 6:1). This is the term to which the sinner comes back. Sin is a departing from God, repentance is a coming back to him again. It is a coming back, like that of a runaway servant to his master, returning to his place and duty in the family. Sin carried away mankind from God two ways:

1. Sin carried men away from God as a portion in which to rest. He is all-sufficient to himself and to his creatures, and none but he is so. Sin carried man away from God to the creatures for happiness and satisfaction: hence says Jehovah, 'My people have committed two evils: they have forsaken me the fountain of living waters, and hewed them out cisterns, broken cisterns, that can hold no water' (Jer. 2:13). There he seeks a rest to his heart. By faith man returns to God as a portion, unites with him again through Christ, and takes everlasting rest in him. He returns as the dove to the ark, 'Who are these that fly as a cloud, and as the doves to their windows?' (Isa. 60:8).

2. Sin carried man away from God as a Lord and Master, to whom he owes obedience. In this respect man returns to God by repentance, returning to his duty (Ps. 119:9). Men turning from God, turn their backs on his laws, and make their own lusts their laws; but the repenting sinner

turns back to the laws of God (Ps. 119:59). He has slipped his neck out of the yoke of the commands of Christ, but he comes and takes it on again, never to throw it off anymore (Matt. 11:29). He has gone off the road, the strait way; but he comes back, and bids an eternal farewell to the broad way.

Without reluctance

A return of the soul to God himself (1 Kings 18:37), consisting in the heart's turning to the loving and liking of the Lord as a Lord and Master. Sinners departing from God, not only mislike their service, but the Master and his house, 'His citizens hated him, and sent a message after him, saying, We will not have this man to reign over us' (Luke 19:14). They are filled with prejudices against him, there is a natural aversion in the heart to him, they cannot away with subjection to him. Hence 'they say to God, Depart from us; for we desire not the knowledge of your ways' (Job 21:14). But in repentance that aversion is cured, and the soul inclines and moves towards him in heart and affections. This consists in three things.

The soul is brought to esteem the Lord worthy to be served and pleased in all things. The name of God is to the penitent a worthy name (James 2:7). The soul sees the transcendent glory and excellency of God, worthy of all adoration and obedience; and so slights and disdains all other masters, as unworthy of the service of an immortal soul.

The soul chooses him as its only Lord and Master, saying, 'O Lord our God, other lords besides you have had dominion over us: but by you only will we make mention of your name' (Isa. 26:13). This was Joshua's choice, 'As for me and my house, we will serve the Lord' (Josh. 24:15). The enlightened mind beholds his glory, the glory and excellency of himself, his image, laws, ordinances, and service; and the renewed will consents and cleaves to him. It has tried many masters, 'serving divers lusts' (Titus 3:3); but could never have satisfaction in the service of any of them, and therefore says, 'I will go and return to my first husband, for then was it better with me than now' (Hosea 2:7).

The soul looks upon the service of God as its great happiness. Hence said the prodigal, when he came to himself, 'How many hired servants of my father's have bread enough and to spare, and I perish with hunger?' (Luke 15:17). And therefore the saints are found declaring them happy who are most employed in his service, as the queen of Sheba said of Solomon's servants: 'Blessed is the man whom you choosest, and causest to approach to you, that he may dwell in your courts' (Ps. 65:4). And, 'Blessed are they that dwell in your house: they will be still praising you' (Ps. 84:4). And till the soul come to this, to account the Lord's service the only true freedom and happiness, though they may take up his service, they will not abide with it, because they do not like their Master.

Embracing duty

There is in this returning a return of the soul to its duty to God. Hence said Saul, 'Lord, what will you have me to do?' (Acts 9:6). Whoever returns to God, comes home as a servant to enter to work: for idlers about God's house may be nominal servants, but real ones they cannot be. God's servants have higher relations which they stand in to him; but all of them have duty annexed to them. Are they married to Christ? They must bring forth fruit (Rom. 7:4). Are they friends? They must do whatsoever he commands them (John 15:14; see Mal. 1:6). Now, the penitent returns to his duty in these two respects.

The penitent returns to his duty *in his heart*. He is reconciled to the whole law of God, and the whole yoke of Christ, so far as it is known to him to be his law and yoke (Ps. 119:6). 'I have respect to all your commandments.' He has a love and liking of the duties of piety towards God, and righteousness towards men. Though there remain in him a contradicting principle, yet he can say, 'I delight in the law of God, after the inward man' (Rom. 7:22). The heart-enmity against the law and the power of godliness is removed, and nothing is so desirable to him as to be holy as God is holy.

He has a full and fixed purpose of new obedience: 'O Lord, I have said, that I would keep your words' (Ps. 119:57). 'I have inclined my ear to perform your statutes alway, even to the end' (Ps. 119:112). He returns with a purpose never to be what he has been; to pursue holiness, to enter upon and keep the way of duty, whatever be the hardships and difficulties he may meet with in it. And this purpose is for to-day, not for to-morrow only; not to delay a minute, but presently to fall in with every known duty, as knowing there is no time for delaying.

The penitent returns to his duty *in both heart and life.* He is brought to sincere endeavours after new obedience:

> Behold, this self-same thing, that you sorrowed after a godly sort, what carefulness it wrought in you, yea, what clearing of yourselves, yea, what indignation, yea, what fear, yea, what vehement desire, yea, what zeal, yea, what revenge! In all things you have approved yourselves to be clear in this matter. (2 Cor.7:11)

Purposes without endeavours are fair blossoms without fruit, which will never prove a penitent. If the lame man be cured, though not perfectly, he will rise and walk as he can. It is true, while here we can do nothing perfectly; but the true penitent will endeavour to do all, and aim at perfection. Hence said Paul, 'I press toward the mark, for the prize of the high calling of God in Christ Jesus' (Phil. 3:14).

1. The penitent returning to his duty returns to the practice of every known duty. Hence said David, 'I have respect to all your commandments' (Ps. 119:6). He labours to know what is duty, and is willing to know it; and when known, endeavours to perform it. He puts hand to external and internal obedience; to serve God in heart and life too; to perform his duty to God and to his neighbour; personal and relative, secret, private, and public.

2. He returns to spirituality in every duty: 'For we are the circumcision, which worship God in the Spirit, and rejoice in Christ Jesus, and have no confidence in the flesh' (Phil. 3:3). The true penitent will not sist in the carcase of duties, but will endeavour to get in to those unseen things where lies the life and soul of duties; namely, to have his heart imbued with love to God as the principle of his obedience, touched with regard to the honour of God as his end, raised above selfish ends and designs, and performing all in faith, leaning on the Lord for strength.

'I will arise and go to my father…'

A *sincere* returning, not feigned and hypocritical, with the whole heart (Jer. 3:10). Hypocrites are said to have a heart and a heart, a divided heart, one for God, and another for their lusts. But the Lord says in this case, If you take me, let these go away. For no man can serve two masters. It is a returning to him to abide with him for ever, as Onesimus to Philemon (v. 15). The penitent, like the servant under the law, his ear is nailed to God's door-posts, to serve him for ever. To return for a time is naught.

A *voluntary* return. The penitent comes back with heart and good-will, 'Your people will be willing in the day of your power' (Ps. 110:3). As one that is going back to a good and honourable master, and will serve him with gladness: 'Serve the Lord with gladness' (Ps. 100:2). They that are only driven back to God, by heavy rods or sharp convictions, will come away again; yet people may be driven at first to God, who seeing his glory and excellency, and the desirableness of his service afterwards, do voluntarily and heartily yield themselves to him.

A *speedy* return: 'I made haste, and delayed not to keep your commandments' (Ps. 119:60). They that are sincere will not delay for a moment; they will make no truce with sin. The moment in which true repentance touches the heart, is the precise term of going home to God; for they know that if they delay a moment longer, that moment may be the fatal moment to them.

A *thorough* return. The soul sticks at known duty, but embraces all, be it ever so hard, and unpleasant to flesh and blood. Hence said the Lord of David, 'I have found David the son of Jesse; a man after my own heart, which will fulfil all my will' (Acts 13:22). The penitent puts a blank in God's hand, saying, 'Lord, what will you have me to do? Speak, Lord,' says he, 'your servant hears.' He is for the will of God, without disputing. For God is an absolute master, and is therefore to be obeyed without reserve.

Using the Truth

> This point lets us see that negative reformation is not sufficient for repentance. One must not only turn from sin, but turn to God. We must not only put away evil, but take in to us the contrary good: 'Wash and make yourselves clean, put away the evil of your doings from before my eyes, cease to do evil, learn to do well' (Isa. 1: 16). We must not only give up with such and such lusts, but be endued with the contrary graces. Some people reform from the evils of their life, but they do not go forward to the positive ways of holiness. They satisfy themselves, with the proud Pharisee, that they are not unjust, no extortioners; but they do not consider, that when the house which the devil goes out of is empty, he returns with seven spirits more wicked than himself, and so the last state of such a person is worse than the first (Matt. 12: 44–5).

3

Repent!

I come now to the application of the whole. And here I would sound the alarm in the ears of impenitent sinners, to repent, and turn from their sins to God. O sinners, repent, repent; you are gone away to your lusts and idols, turn from them; you have turned your back on God, turn to him again.

You Need to Repent

I will endeavour to convince you of the need you have to repent, to make way for the motives to it. Three sorts of persons will readily stave off all our calls to repentance.

Three Excuses

One says, I repent of my sins daily. Well were it with you, if it were so. Surely there is need for it. But none are so ready to pretend to this, as those that never yet knew what it is to repent. If ruing the ill you have done, a sigh for it, and a short-winded wish for mercy, be repentance, it is easy work. But it is not so. You cannot repent with a hale heart: that heart of yours must be rent for sin, and rent from it; you must turn from sin to God in all known duties of obedience. If you pretend then to repentance, bring forth fruits meet for it. But to such pretended penitents we may say, as Samuel to Saul, 'What means then this bleating of the sheep, and the lowing of the oxen?' (1 Sam. 15:14).

Another says, I have repented already. But O consider, repentance is not the work of a day, but of your whole lifetime, since you are never free of sin (Jer. 8:6). New provocations require new repentance; no, old sins are not to be forgotten. Hence said Moses, 'Remember, and forget not how you provoked the Lord your God to wrath in the wilderness' (Deut. 9:7). And hence prays the Psalmist, 'Remember not the sins of my youth, nor my transgressions' (Ps. 25:7). And if you repent of them thoroughly, you will be ashamed, and the wound will bleed afresh at the remembrance of them. Hence said the apostle, 'What fruit had you in those things, of which you are now ashamed?' (Rom. 6:21).

Another sees no need of repentance for him; for such persons are of that blinded generation that are pure in their own eyes, and yet is not washed from their filthiness (Prov. 30:12). They deny their sin instead of mourning over and confessing it, saying, 'I have done no wickedness' (Prov. 30:20). They possibly keep free from the gross pollutions of the outward man; and for the positive duties of religion, they either see no need of them, or if they do perform them too, they are blind to the corruption of their nature, and to heart sins, and the spirituality of the law of God. But you need repentance as much as the proud Pharisee (Luke 18) and as the Apostle Paul (Rom. 7:9; compared with Titus 3).

Think Again

Are there not many of us that never got a sound awakening all their days? They had lived under the sound of the gospel, but it never broke their rest effectually in a sinful course. I will read the mystery of your case: 'When a strong man armed keeps his palace, his goods are in peace' (Luke 11:21). Repent then, else you are undone.

Are there not many whose awakening has produced a partial change on them, but it has ended in a fearful apostasy from the way of God? 'It is happened to them according to the true proverb, The dog is turned to his own vomit again; and, the sow that was washed, to her wallowing in the mire' (2 Pet. 2:22). Their fair blossom they once had, has gone up as dust. Repent, or your backsliding will be your ruin.

Are there not many sleeping virgins at this day, who are in a course of departing from God? The life, vigour, and tenderness they sometimes had, is gone; and death has settled down on their eyelids, and they are turned to be of the colour of the earth. To these we must say, 'Remember therefore from whence you are fallen, and repent, and do the first works' (Rev. 2:5).

Are there not many living in known sin? They know the particulars in which they are wrong, and yet on they go, as an ox to the slaughter. Their corruptions are too strong for conscience. You must repent, or you will perish. Profane courses will make a miserable end, and one sin retained will ruin the soul.

Look and see whether you can perceive the footsteps of Christ's flock, or of the devil's drove, on the way which you are going (Song 1:8). Is your case the case in which the fair company walked with displayed banners to Canaan, or that in which many have slept and slipped away to the pit?

Can you deny but that there are many foul steps you have made and are making? O then repent. Go no farther on; one step more may put you beyond returning (Luke 14:24). Little knows the sinner how soon God may take the foot from him, either by clapping a withering curse on him, as on the fig-tree (Mark 11:14), or by taking him red-hand in his sin, and sending him to the pit. 'He that being often reproved, hardens his neck, will suddenly be destroyed, and that without remedy' (Prov. 29:1).

Why You Need to Repent

I will lay before you a train of motives to repentance. Consider the obligations that lie on you to repent. Sit down and consider how manifold ties are on you to it.

You Are Under Several Obligations

The *command of God* obliges you to it: 'God commanded all men everywhere to repent' (Acts 17:30). And will you not have regard to the sovereign authority of him that made you? The command to repentance is one of the two great commands of the gospel, 'Testifying both to the Jews, and also to the Greeks, repentance toward God, and faith toward our Lord Jesus Christ' (Acts 20:21). This is the command which the prophets of old did so often inculcate, 'Repent, and turn yourselves from all your transgressions; so iniquity will not be your ruin' (Ezek. 18:30). This our Lord Jesus and the Baptist preached, and his disciples, saying, 'Repent, for the kingdom of heaven is at hand.' This the Apostles preached, 'Repent, and be baptized every one of you in the name of Jesus Christ, for the remission of sins' (Acts 2:38). And this all along is the joint sound of the preachers of the gospel. So it is an old and new command too. No command is more peremptorily laid on, as in the text. As you regard then God's authority, repent.

Your *baptism* obliges you: 'John did baptize in the wilderness, and preach the baptism of repentance, for the remission of sins' (Mark 1:4). It is a solemn tie laid upon you to return to and serve God the Father, Son, and Holy Ghost; to die to sin, to live to righteousness. You have then taken on the Lord's badge; how dreadful must it be to continue runaways from your Great Master? Repent, then, and return, as you would not be treated as runaways from your colours, as rebels that cast off your allegiance sworn to the King of heaven.

Your *mercies* oblige you in point of gratitude, 'Do you despise the riches of his goodness, and forbearance, and long-suffering; not knowing that the goodness of God leads you to repentance?' (Rom. 2:4). Your common mercies, and special ones, preventing, restraining. Every mercy is forfeited by sin; yet you are still in God's debt, and every day a new load of favours is laid on, and these are strong ties to repentance.

Your *profession* obliges you. You profess yourselves as Christians. If you will name the name of Christ, then depart from iniquity (2 Tim. 2:19). Why do you call God Father, if you will needs do the works of the devil (John 8:44), which Christ came to destroy? Do you profess Christ your Redeemer, the Holy Ghost your Sanctifier? Why then do you continue in bondage to your sin, in unholy courses? Do you believe every sin deserves God's wrath? What madness is it then to be treasuring up wrath against the day of wrath. Quit your profession then, or quit your sinful courses.

Sin Will Cost You Everything
Seriously consider what sin is, that you are so fond of, prefer to Christ, and for the enjoyment of it forfeit the favour of

God. What do you see in it, that does so powerfully charm you? If you are taken with the profit of it, you would consider that no advantage will quit the cost of the soul's ruin brought about by it: 'For what is a man profited, if he will gain the whole world, and lose his own soul? Or what will a man give in exchange for his soul?' (Matt. 16:26). 'For what is the hope of the hypocrite, though he has gained, when God takes away his soul?' (Job 27:8). If you are taken with the pleasure of it; that is dear bought, being purchased at the rate of eternal flames, which sin will bring me to without repentance. The pleasures of sin are but momentary (Heb. 11:25). And there is far more in God's service, even in this world: 'There be many that say, Who will show us any good? Lord, lift you up the light of your countenance upon us. You have put gladness in my heart, more than in the time that their corn and their wine increased' (Ps. 4:6-7).

Has not every bait a hook with it? (Prov. 23:31-2). Is there not a trap, gin, and snare in them all for you? How often have you seen there has been death in the pot, when you have sat down to feed your corruptions? You have snatched at the bait, but have you not in the meantime felt yourselves wounded with the hook? You have smelled the rose, but have not the prickles meanwhile annoyed you? And how can it be otherwise? For 'he that digs a pit, will fall into it; and whoever breaks an hedge, a serpent will bite him' (Eccles. 10:8).

Is there any solid rest in a sinful course? No, surely: 'There is no peace, says my God, to the wicked' (Isa. 57:21). Do not your consciences witness, that the sting of guilt in the conscience is like a dead fly in the ointment, causing all to be unsavoury? Is there not always a worm at the root of every sinful gourd you sit down under the shadow of? Do not the very maybees of conscience suck the sap out of your lusts many times? Will any man say, that ever he found rest to his soul in a course of departing from God? No, no; ten thousand worlds will not satisfy an immortal soul.

Do not you find sin to be *an insatiable tyrant*, like the grave and the barren womb, never saying, It is enough? 'The wicked are like the troubled sea, when it cannot rest, whose waters cast up mire and dirt' (Isa. 57:20). O but they have a hard task, that have living raging lusts to feed! 'You lust, and have not: you kill and desire to have, and cannot obtain: you fight and war, yet you have not, because you ask not. You ask, and receive not, because you ask amiss, that you may consume it upon your lusts' (James 4:2-3). 'And they tempted God in their heart, by asking meat for their lust. Yea, they spoke against God: they said, Can God furnish a table in the wilderness?' (Ps. 78:18-19). The more they are indulged, the more they grow rampant: the more their thirst is cared for, the greater thirst is created. Hence men in a sinful course go from evil to worse.

Is not a sinful course a *most foolish course?* No man is unfaithful to God, but he is unfaithful to himself, and his own interest and happiness. The Lord offers to reason the matter with you, and to make your consciences judge; 'Come now, and let us reason together, says the Lord: though your sins be as scarlet, they will be as white as snow; though they be red like crimson, they will be as wool' (Isa. 1:18). It stands between you, and temporal and eternal happiness. It is a poisonous cup, bringing death along with it. And how foolish is it for men to hug a serpent in their bosom, when called to throw it out; to drink a cup of poison, when called to throw it away; to take coals in their bosom, when it is told they will burn them; to court their own death and ruin?

Is not sin *the separation wall between God and you?* 'Your iniquities have separated between you and your God, and your sins have hid his face from you, that he will not hear' (Isa. 59:2). Does it not mar your comfort from the word, your confidence in the Lord, and your access to God in duties? Does it not make as it were a gulf between heaven and you, that whatever communion others have with heaven, your unrepented-of sins let you have none? Shall this be your choice? Sure, then, you need not wonder, if you will not come back to God, he bid you at last depart from him, 'into everlasting fire, prepared for the devil and his angels.'

Consider what will be *the end of sin.* Surely it will be bitterness in the end: 'Your own wickedness will correct you, and your backsliding will reprove you: know therefore and see, that it is an evil thing and bitter, that you have forsaken the Lord your God, and that my fear is not in you, says the Lord God of hosts' (Jer. 2:19). However pleasant the cup seem to be at the brim, the dregs of it will be bitter: 'Stolen waters are sweet, and bread eaten in secret is pleasant. But he knows not that the dead are there; and that her guests are in the depths of hell' (Prov. 9:17-18). However taking the entertainment be, the reckoning will be dreadful.

You Must Die

'It is appointed to men once to die' (Heb. 9:27). Death is certain, and therefore repentance is necessary. O if men would realise death to themselves, sinners would soon find it necessary to turn a new leaf. One hearing Genesis 5 read in the church, was so impressed with the thoughts of death, that he presently betook himself to a new course of life, that he might die well. We must all meet with death, lie down in the grave; let us view it beforehand, and see how it calls us to repent. Look to your dying hour, and to your grave, O impenitent sinner, and consider these few things.

Would you be content to die *as you live?* You live in your sin, without God; would you desire to die so? Many indeed entertain Balaam's wish, for the death of the righteous, while they care not for their life, 'Let me die the death of the righteous, and let my last end be like his' (Num. 23:10). But remember he did not get it, 'Balaam also the son of Beor they slew with the sword' (Num. 31:8). And while death is so uncertain, it is the hanging of an eternal weight on a hair, to look to get matters mended then, that are not mended now.

What will a sinful life look like *on a deathbed?* How will you be able to look your unrepented-of guilt and a long eternity in the face together? 'Can your heart endure, or can your hands be strong in the days that I will deal with you? I the Lord have spoken it, and will do it' (Ezek. 22:14). Sin sits easy now on a sleepy conscience, while health and strength lasts, and death appears not. But when death stares you in the face, and the awakened conscience flies upon you, it will cut you to the heart, that you have not repented before.

What will it be to die, and go to another world *with a load of unrepented-of guilt on your back?* Look to your grave beforehand; think with yourselves, how will it be to lie down there with your bones full of your iniquity? Is it not best now, to shake off and cast away your transgressions, as knowing that however you may live with them, you cannot die with them well.

At a dying hour you must *part with the world*, and the enjoyment of your lusts. The foul feast you sit at now, death will overthrow the table, and the sad reckoning for it comes in then, and continues for ever. O rise up now, and leave it by repentance. Part with these things at God's call, which you must part with before long, whether you will or not.

There is *no repentance in the grave* (Eccles. 9:10). You must repent, or you perish; and it is now or never. Mar matters now by an impenitent life, and let death catch you there, you will never be able to mend them more. The working time, and time of trial is over then. If the brittle thread of life were broke, which may be snapped asunder in a moment, then you are beyond the line of mercy. The candle burnt to snuff, will be as soon brought to burn again, as time will be recalled.

Judgment Is Coming
Take a view of the tribunal of God, before which you must appear: 'We must all appear before the judgment seat of Christ; that every one may receive the things done in his body, according to that he has done, whether it be good or bad. Knowing therefore the terror of the Lord, we persuade men' (2 Cor. 5:10-11). O sinner, do you not know that there is a judgment to come, and how this calls you to repent? 'God commands all men everywhere to repent: because he has appointed a day, in the which he will judge the world in righteousness, by that man whom he has ordained: of which he has given assurance to all men, in that he has raised him from the dead' (Acts 17:30-31). Were men to lie for ever neglected, without a future reckoning, as the beasts that perish, they might live as they desire, the hazard of condemnation for an eternity would not press them. But it is not so: 'it is appointed to men once to die, but after this the judgment' (Heb. 9:27).

While you are going on in sin, your debt to the divine justice is increasing, the accounts are swelling; and the reckoning for them before the tribunal will be terrible, however little you think of them now (Eccles. 11:9). They may fall out of your memory, but they will not fall out of the book of God's remembrance (Hosea 13:12). But now is the time to get them laid over on the cautioner's score.

Though you will not seek them out now to mourn over them, and turn from them, they will find you out before the tribunal of God. Happy would the sinner be, if his sins would part with him at the grave; but they 'will lie down with him in the dust' (Job 20:11): or if they would lie down with him there, if they would lie still and never rise again; but 'God will bring every work into judgment, with every secret thing, whether it be good, or whether it be evil' (Eccles. 12:14). The Judge is omniscient, nothing can be hid from him, he is not capable to forget the least injury which the sinner has to his glory; all must come into the account.

When you see Christ come again, and his throne set for judgment, when the trumpet will blow, and the dead arise, and made to appear before that tribunal, when the heavens and earth will pass away, what will be your thoughts of staving off repentance?

Your state for eternity will be determined according to your deeds done in the flesh. Impenitent sinners will get a long eternity to rue their obstinancy in, while those that repented in time shall be happy for ever.

Christ Suffered for Sin

To move you to repentance, consider the sufferings of Christ. A Roman senator intending to provoke the people to revenge the death of Caesar killed by Brutus, brought forth his bloody robe and cried, 'Here is the robe of your late emperor.' And O will you look to the bloody robe of Christ, hung up on the pole of the gospel, to move you to repentance? 'They will look upon me whom they have pierced, and they will mourn for him' (Zech. 12:10).

How dreadful must God's indignation against sin be, which is written with the blood of Christ, pierced with the sword of justice. Is it not 'a fearful thing to fall into the hands of the living God'? And will we continue in sin, against which such indignation appeared?

Sin appeared terrible in Sodom when in flames, but yet more terrible in mount Calvary, where the justice of God pursued the Son of God with the sword of vengeance. A spectacle of amazement, the Son of God set up for a mark to the arrows of God! Do you not ask into the cause of all this? It was sin. The children ate the sour grape, and the father's teeth were set on edge. They contract the debt, justice lays hold on him, and he 'restores what he took not away' (Ps. 69:4). The elect took on the debt jovially, but he is put to tears and strong cries in the paying of it. And will we not hate and loathe sin?

Many waters cannot quench love, neither can the floods from above nor from below drown it. 'Behold how he loved you.' He might have been happy in his Father's love, though mortals never shared of it with him. But such was his love to sinners, as made him lay down his life for them, that so a way might be paved for the egress of his Father's love towards them. And will you not hate and loathe sin which was the cause of death? Is this your kindness to your friend?

When Christ suffered, the earth quaked, rocks rent, the dead arose, the sun was struck blind with the sight, and hid his face for shame: and how can we stand unmoved, who were the first movers of the bloody tragedy, whose sins furnished Judas to betray him, a Pilate to sentence him? Look here, and mourn for, and turn from sin.

Did he not suffer enough? Must he suffer more still, even in his state of exaltation? Will you grieve his Spirit, trample on his laws, yea and his blood, continuing impenitent in your sins?

You Wrong God

Consider the wrong done to God by your sin, in which you may see the ugly picture of it. This kept Joseph from yielding to a strong temptation (Gen. 39:9); and pierced David's heart with repentance for his sin (Ps. 51:4); and lay heavy on the prodigal son (Luke 15:18). Every sin reaches the throne of God in heaven, and him that sits on it. It is true, the malice of sinners against God is impotent malice, and can do him no real prejudice, do their worst. They cannot make him less happy, they cannot disturb his peace (Job 35:6-8). But the sinner is like the beggar full of sores lying on a dunghill, venting his spite against the prince on the throne. He wrongs the honour of God, his declarative glory, though he can do nothing against his essential glory. Sinner, you wrong God by your sin.

By setting yourself in opposition to his nature and will. What is sin continued in without repentance? 'A walking contrary to God' (Lev. 26:21); an interpretative aim to throw him down from his sovereignty, 'The fool has said in his heart, There is no God' (Ps. 14:1). You may put what fair colours you please upon it; but it is a throwing out the flag of defiance against the God that made you. For do you not thereby in effect disregard his all-seeing eye, and presence everywhere, bid defiance to his justice, and call in question his truth, despise his goodness and mercy, and run counter to his holy nature and will, while you run still on that of which he has said, 'Oh do not this abominable thing that I hate!' (Jer. 44:4). And is this a course to be insisted in?

You wrong God *by trampling on his laws* (Isa. 33:22). He has given you a law to be the rule of your life, he has stamped it with his own sovereign authority, fenced it with punishments threatened, suitable to his infinite greatness: but you make no more of these than if they were cobwebs fit only to catch flies. You break through the fences, and in comtempt of his authority, will be over into the forbidden ground. Thus you affront the God that made you: will he sit with it think you? No, he can avenge the affront, 'There is one lawgiver, who is able to save and to destroy;' and he will do it (James 4:12); 'Those my enemies which would not that I should reign over them, bring hither, and slay them before me' (Luke 19:27).

You wrong God *by despising his Son* (John 5:40). You wrong God at the rate heathens cannot do, and therefore your condemnation will be greater than theirs (John 3:19). God has sent his Son into the world, by his death to procure reconciliation between God and sinners; he has 'exalted him to give repentance' (Acts 5:31): but by your continuing in sin, you slight his death, and the purchase of his blood: you love your disease so, as you loathe the Physician. What will be the end of these things? 'Behold, you despisers, and wonder, and perish' (Acts 13:41).

You wrong God *by grieving his Spirit* (Eph. 4:30). Hear God's complaints of impenitent sinners, 'I am broken with their whorish heart which has departed from me, and with their eyes which go a whoring after their idols' (Ezek. 6:9). 'Behold, I am pressed under you, as a cart is pressed that is full of sheaves' (Amos 2:13). How often has the Spirit of the Lord been at work with you to turn you from your sins, speaking to you by the work, providences, the secret checks of your own conscience, and secret motions and whispers within your own breast, but all to no purpose? This will not last: 'And the Lord said, My spirit will not always strive with man, for that he also is flesh' (Gen. 6:3). And it will have a doleful end, if you do not repent: 'They rebelled, and vexed his holy Spirit: therefore he was turned to be their enemy, and he fought against them' (Isa. 58:10). If sinners continue to be a burden to the Spirit of God, and do not take off the burden by repentance, God will throw it off to their cost: 'Therefore says the Lord, the Lord of hosts, the mighty One of Israel, Ah, I will ease me of my adversaries, and avenge me of my enemies' (Isa. 1:24).

You wrong God *by defacing the remains of his image* in your own soul, God made man upright, after his own image. Adam's sin ruined his image in us. But the more we go on and sin, we render ourselves still the more unlike God, and the more contrary to him. How fearful is this, to be blotting out any appearance of the traits of God's image in us?

You wrong God *by the ill influence your example has on others*. Hence says our Lord, 'Because iniquity will abound, the love of many will wax cold' (Matt. 24:12). Every impenitent sinner is an agent for the devil, and invites and encourages others to despise God and his ways, and so will be made to reckon for the mischief his sin does that way. The rich man in hell was sensible of this, though it would seem not before, 'I pray you, father,' said he to Abraham, 'that you would send him [Lazarus] to my father's house: for I have five brethren; that he may testify to them, lest they also come into this place of torment' (Luke 16:27-8).

Now, will you go on, thus wronging God by your sin, and not turn from it to him?

He is *your Creator* (Eccles. 12:1). He gave you a being, and brought you out of the womb of nothing, and will you not be for him? Will you be against him? Has not he that made you a right to rule you? Does not reason itself say, that God's creating us gives him a sovereign dominion over us? O why will the creature thus set itself against the Creator? Will the potsherds strive against the potter.

He is *your Preserver* (Heb. 1:3. Acts 17:28). You live on his earth, feed on his good creatures, breathe in his air, and will you not hearken to his voice? Who was it that preserved you in the womb, that brought you out of it, so that it was not made your grave? Who has kept the brittle thread of your life from being broken hitherto, and fed you all your life long? Is it not the Lord? And will you fight against him with his own benefits which he has bestowed on you, yea, is bestowing on you while you go on in your sin? Shall the life, strength, comforts of life, time, which he has given you, be employed to the grieving of his Spirit? What will the end of these things be?

He can destroy you, and that when he will (Matt. 10:28). Your life and breath are from him, and he can stop them when he pleases. He does not suffer you to go on in your sin, because he cannot help it, no, the moment you provoke him, he can strike you dead, or send you down alive into the pit. But he waits to be gracious. And this one consideration might determine sinners to repent, if madness were not in their hearts, setting them to provoke him, who in a moment can destroy them, and make them silent in the grave.

He is *your Witness* (Ps. 51:4; Luke 15:18). Sinners that like not to retain God in their knowledge, do in effect please themselves with the notion that God is closed up in heaven, 'For they say, The Lord has forsaken the earth, and the Lord sees not' (Ezek. 9:9). But the day comes when they will see themselves miserably deceived. No; he is a witness, though many times a silent witness; but he will speak in due time

(Ps. 50:21-2). The opening of the book of conscience, and of God's remembrance, will clear his being a witness of your whole way and every step of it.

He will be *your Judge* (2 Cor. 5:10). And he is an omniscient one, from whom nothing can be hid; a just one, that will reward every one according to his works; an omnipresent one, from whose presence there can be no escape; an omnipotent one who can without fail make his sentence take effect. Will men pretend to believe a judgment to come, and yet be at no pains to make the judge their friend beforehand, but keep up the war against him, and not break it off by repentance? Alas! horrid unbelief is at the bottom of impenitency.

God Calls You to Turn

God is calling you to repentance. Be not deaf to the calls of God, lest the Lord pay home your rebellion, by refusing to hear you when you call to him (Prov. 1:24-8). God is calling you to repentance:

By the mercies wherewith he is daily loading you. 'Do you despise the riches of his goodness, and forbearance, and long-suffering; not knowing that the goodness of God leads you to repentance?' (Rom. 2:4). These are the cords of a man wherewith God is drawing you. That you are spared on God's earth, that you are kept out of hell, that he gives you daily bread, and does not lock up heaven and earth that they may not help you, call aloud to you to repent, and turn to him. And he takes notice of how little these prevail, 'Neither say they in their heart, Let us now fear the Lord our God that gives rain, both the former and the latter in his season: he reserves to us the appointed weeks of the harvest' (Jer. 5:24).

God is calling you to repentance *by the crosses and afflictions*, either laid on you, or threatened. Every cross providence is a messenger from heaven calling you to repentance: 'Hear you the rod, and who has appointed it' (Micah 6:9). They meet you in the way of sin, as the angel did Balaam; they bid you halt, and go no farther on; no, they bid you return to the Lord. God is speaking to the land this way, to this church, and to the congregation, and to everyone of us at this day.

God is calling you to repentance *by the preaching of the word* (Acts 17:30). This is the great scope of all our preaching, that you may repent and turn from your sins to God. And while God continues his gospel with us, it is a sign he is waiting for our repentance: but to continue in sin over the belly of all warnings, will have a fatal end to take us from the gospel, or the gospel from us; which we have ground to fear at this day on more accounts than one. Hence says Christ to the church of Ephesus, 'Remember from whence you are fallen, and repent, and do the first works; or else I will come to you quickly, and will remove your candlestick out of his place, unless you repent' (Rev. 2:5).

If You Do not Repent, You Will Perish

Sin unrepented of, brings ruin upon kingdoms, churches, congregations, families. And that is like to be the ruin of our land, and of our church, at this day. For the face of all at this day is like that described. 'I hearkened and heard, but they spoke not aright: no man repented him of his wickedness, saying, What have I done? Every one turned to his course, as the horse rushes into the battle' (Jer. 8:6). God has threatened us with desolating strokes, and is yet threatening but the generation is like to those scoffers spoken of saying, 'Where is the promise of his coming?' (2 Pet. 3:4). And because God does not speedily execute the sentence, therefore men cast off fear, and go on in their sins, in defiance of heaven. But that concerns us nearly: 'Shall I not visit them for these things? says the Lord: will not my soul be avenged on such a nation as this?' (Jer. 9:9).

Sin unrepented of will ruin your souls; unless you repent, you will perish. Consider, your life, your souls lie at stake. Sinner, you have gone away from God, your soul is left in pawn that you will return by repentance. If you return not, your pawn, your soul is lost, lost for ever. Heaven's gate is too narrow to let you in there with a burden of unrepented-of sin on your back. No, heaven you can never see; hell you cannot escape, if you repent not. The gospel calls you to repent; if not, 'the Lord Jesus will be revealed from heaven, with his mighty angels, in flaming fire, taking vengeance on you that know not God, and that obey not the gospel of our Lord Jesus Christ' (2 Thess. 1:7-8). Have pity therefore on your souls, 'Cast away from you all your transgressions, whereby you have transgressed, and make you a new heart, and a new spirit; for why will you die, O house of Israel? For I have no pleasure in the death of him that dies, says the Lord God: wherefore turn yourselves, and live you' (Ezek. 18:31-2). To this narrow point the matter is brought, repent, or perish eternally; quit your sins, or quit heaven.

Now, I pray you *consider the certainty of your ruin* in an impenitent state. You have it from the mouth of the Lord himself, in most plain and peremptory terms, that 'unless you repent, you will perish.' If it were but a may-be, it were sufficient in all reason to determine us to repentance; for it is unaccountable to put the soul in hazard of everlasting destruction, for all the profit or pleasure of a sinful course;

a thousand times more than for one to put himself in hazard of drowning to catch a fly. But it is not a may-be, but certainly it will be.

All other grounds of hope are cut off, if you repent not. Tell me, O impenitent sinner, that will not turn from your sin, what will you trust for salvation from the wrath of God? Will you trust to the mercy of God? I tell you, you are a despiser of mercy (Rom. 2:4); and you cannot have it in this case, but over the belly of the truth of God; for he has said, 'Unless you repent, you will perish.' Pray consider, if you would have mercy, you must seek it in God's way: 'Let the wicked forsake his way, and the unrighteous man his thoughts: and let him return to the Lord, and he will have mercy upon him, and to our God, for he will abundantly pardon' (Isa. 55:7).

Will you trust to Jesus Christ, his blood and merits? Do not deceive yourself. Is this not Christ's own word, 'Unless you repent you will perish'? Does not the Saviour tell you this? None of my blood will ever be wared on a sinner to save him from wrath, that will not repent and turn from his sin. Why does anybody at all perish that hears the gospel, if folk may continue impenitent, and yet share of Christ's blood? No, no; to whom Christ will be a Saviour from wrath, he will be first a Saviour from sin (Matt. 1:21). He will first give repentance, before he give access to heaven; for Christ's blood was never shed to bring dogs and swine into his Father's house, but shed, 'that he might redeem us from all iniquity, and purify to himself a peculiar people, zealous of good works (Titus 2:14).

Where will the fruit of sin be, when this dear reckoning begins? 'It is a fearful thing to fall into the hands of the living God' (Heb. 10:31). You may get a time to run your course: but at length your eye-strings will break, the last pulse beat, and the soul will take wing and go to another world, and because of unrepented-of sin, be condemned to everlasting flames. And when you enter there, what will abide with you of all the satisfaction you have had in your sinful courses? No; then you must bid an eternal farewell to all satisfaction, ease, or delight whatsoever, either in God or your lusts.

How will you be able to stand under the load of wrath in the pit of destruction? 'The sinners in Zion are afraid, fearfulness has surprised the hypocrites: who among us will dwell with the devouring fire? Who amongst us will dwell with everlasting burnings?' (Isa. 33:14). How will you be able to grapple with vengeance, the Mediator's vengeance, while God will hold you up with the one hand, and punish you with the other? Think in time on the worm that never dies, and the fire that is never quenched: for either you must repent now, or that worm will gnaw you, and that fire scorch you for ever.

Consider the eternity of this state. The pleasure, profit, and ease of sin are but for a moment; but the destruction for sin unrepented of is for ever (2 Thess. 1:9). O madness! To run the risk of everlasting pain for a moment's pleasure! If ruing, sorrow, remorse, rage against one's self for sin, were repenting, there would be repentance enough in hell. Men stave off repentance now for the bitterness of it; but there is a sweet in it too: but then you will have the bitterness of it in full measure, but never taste of the sweetness of it; for then the hopes of mercy are razed; and a fearful sight of an everlasting continuance of misery, without end.

Have pity then on your own souls, and throw them not away for that which cannot profit.

If You Repent, You Will Never Perish

Repentance is the way to keep off the wrath of God from nations and churches. Repentance is the way for each of us to escape the wrath of God: 'Repent, and turn yourselves from all your transgressions; so iniquity will not be your ruin' (Ezek. 18:30). 'Repent, and be baptized every one of you in the name of Jesus Christ, for the remission of sins' (Acts 2:38). All the threatenings of wrath are summons to repent, and have always that clause understood in them, 'Unless you repent, you will perish.' 'Behold, I will cast her into a bed, and them that commit adultery with her into great tribulation, except they repent of their deeds' (Rev. 2:22). Though you have sinned with the world, if you repent with God's elect, you will not perish with the world.

It is not falling into sin, but lying in sin without repentance, that ruins folk to whom the gospel comes (John 3:19). For there is a remedy provided; and it is for all diseases of the soul, even the worst and most desperate: and so nothing can be fatal to those that are willing to employ the Physician, and to undergo his method of cure. They are in glory this day, whose sins have been of the first magnitude, as David, Paul, Manasseh, Peter; but they were repenting sinners.

There is mercy for you, if you will repent, and come to Christ. Good news, O sinners, if you repent, all your sins will be blotted out, you will be embraced in the wide and warm arms of mercy; if, as you have gone away from God, so you will come back again: 'Let the wicked forsake his way, and the unrighteous man his thoughts: and let him return to the Lord, and he will have mercy upon him, and to our God, for he will abundantly pardon' (Isa. 55:7). 'Behold I stand at the door, and knock: if any man hear my voice, and open the door, I will come in to him, and will sup with him, and

Objections and Answers

My sins are many and great sins.

God's mercies are many (Ps. 51:1) and great too (Ps. 86:13); and his mercy is magnified in pardoning of such. If your sins were as great as mountains, as many as the catalogue of them would reach from heaven to earth, there is mercy for you, if you will repent, 'Come now, and let us reason together, says the Lord: though your sins be as scarlet, they will be as white as snow; though they be red like crimson, they will be as wool' (Isa. 1:18). There are riches of mercy (Eph. 2:4), abundance of pardoning grace (Isa. 55:7).

I have relapsed, gone back with the dog to the vomit, and with the sow that was washed, to the wallowing in the mire.

There is mercy for backsliders too: 'Turn, O backsliding children, says the Lord, for I am married to you' (Jer. 3:14). 'Return, you backsliding children, and I will heal your backslidings' (Jer. 3:22). If it were not so, who could be safe? Men must forgive in that case, and much more God will (Luke 17:4). For as the heavens are above the earth, so are God's thoughts above ours: 'They say, If a man put away his wife, and she go from him, and become another man's, will he return to her again? Will not that land be greatly polluted? But you have played the harlot with many lovers; yet return again to me, says the Lord' (Jer. 3:1).

I have despised and slighted mercy, and the remedy of sin.

They had gone all that length, who had so far despised mercy, and the remedy of sin, as they had murdered the Lord of glory, and yet they obtained mercy (Acts 2:36-8). Despise and slight it no more, and your former sins will not be remembered.

I have so long gone on in sin, that I can have no hope.

The longer the greater is your sin; yet God has not discovered to us any particular time, beyond which he will not wait. There are some called at the eleventh hour; and those that come in then, are not rejected. So was the thief on the cross (Ezek. 33:10-11; Luke 14:22; Joel 3:21).

Nobody's case is like mine.

Consider the case of Manasseh (2 Chron. 33): and of Paul (1 Tim. 1:13). Such instances are designed to encourage sinners to repent in hope of mercy (Eph. 2:7). Adam's case was more hopeless, who had sinned against more light and mercy, than you were capable to do. But suppose your case is a non-such evil, the mercy of God and the blood of Christ are non-such remedies. And you may be sure, since he has said, 'Him that comes to me, I will in no wise cast out' (John 6:37) that he will work a new thing on the earth, rather than that your case be unhelped, if you will put it in his hand. There is mercy for you, if you will repent.

he with me' (Rev. 3:20). O sirs, will not bowels of mercy draw you? God is now on a throne of mercy; he stretches out the golden sceptre to you for peace, if you will have it in his own way: and in his name we proclaim mercy to all poor sinners that desire to turn from their sins to God. O will not the proclamation of the indemnity touch the hearts of rebel sinners, and cause them to relent?

You will certainly be saved for ever, if you repent: 'Repent, and turn yourself from all your transgressions; so iniquity will not be your ruin' (Ezek. 18:30). No true penitents go to hell. Heaven is the landing-place of all true penitents. They that turn from their sins now, and turn to God, will for ever be with the Lord in another world.

O look to the glory that is above, and let your souls be moved to repentance by it. Cast not away the hope of eternal happiness for what does not profit.

Impenitence Is Fatal

Now, sinners, consider these things, and be stirred up to repentance, and do not adventure over the belly of fair warning to go on in a course of impenitency. Impenitency under the gospel is a sin of a deep dye; beware of it.

It is a continuation of sin; it draws out the thread of a God-providing course, adding sin to sin, till God cut the thread of life. Are there not enough items in God's accounts against you already? Why will you add more, instead of diminishing and breaking off the course by repentance?

It seals sin and guilt on your soul. Impenitency keeps all the rest of your sins fast on your souls: 'This is the condemnation, that light is come into the world, and men loved darkness rather than light, because their deeds were evil' (John 3:19). If you would repent, no sins whatsoever you are guilty of should ever be able to ruin you: but if you do not, that one will keep all the rest in life and vigour, to your utter ruin.

It flies in the face of the gospel, of Christ himself, his apostles and ministers, who with one voice call sinners to repentance. If you do this, you do all; if you do not this, you do nothing; you receive the grace of God in vain; it will be in vain to you that ever you heard the gospel, that Christ died for sinners; for you will have no benefit by any of these things.

It is a bloody sin, that will involve you in everlasting misery. For there is no escaping of the wrath of God; if you do not repent, you are undone for ever. For 'unless you repent you will perish.'

Now, you have had a message from the Lord, what answer will I return to him that sent me? I think I may rank up all in these six sorts of sinners.

The brutish sinner, that hears as if he heard not. The work makes a noise in their ears, because they are capable of hearing; but they are no better than the beasts, in so far as they make no reflections on it, with respect to their state and case. What will I say to you, but that the time comes when these souls of yours, drowned in a moss of flesh and blood, will be separate from your bodies, and get a long eternity to reflect on the calls you have had to repent? 'The ox knows his owner, and the ass his master's crib: but Israel does not know, my people do not consider' (Isa. 1:3). 'Be you not as the horse, or as the mule, which have no understanding: whose mouth must be held in with bit and bridle, lest they come near to you. Many sorrows will be to the wicked' (Ps. 32:9-10).

The sullen, desperate sinner, whose answer will be that, 'There is no hope. No, for I have loved strangers, and after them will I go' (Jer. 2:25). Their hearts are glued to their sins, they have no will to part with them, and they have no hope that ever they will be made willing, or if they were so, that God would receive them; and therefore they are resolved to take their time. But I consider, they have been reformed that have been as mad on their idols as you, as Manasseh and Paul. If that cannot draw you, pray answer that question, 'Who among us will dwell with the devouring fire? Who amongst us will dwell with everlasting burnings?' (Isa. 33:14).

The crafty, subtile sinner, whose answer will be that of Saul to Samuel, 'Blessed be you of the Lord: I have performed the commandment of the Lord' (1 Sam. 15:13). But let the return to them be that of Samuel to Saul, 'What means then this bleating of the sheep in my ears, and the lowing of the oxen which I hear?' (1 Sam. 15:14). What means your continuing in sin, your not wrestling and striving against it in heart and life, if it be so?

The presumptuous sinner, whose answer will be that, 'I will have peace, though I walk in the imagination of my heart' (Deut. 29:19). There are some who have a heart of adamant, and put on a forehead of brass, that nothing of this sort can affect them. Let the messengers of the Lord be saying what they will, they will be doing. They will have their course, and persuade themselves all will be well. To such I would say:

> The Lord will not spare him, but then the anger of the Lord, and his jealousy will smoke against that man, and all the curses that are written in this book will lie upon him, and the Lord will blot out his name from under heaven. And the Lord will separate him to evil, out of all the tribes of Israel, according to all the curses of the covenant, that are written in this book of the law. (Deut. 29:20-21)

The slothful sinner, whose answer will be that of Felix to Paul, 'Go your way for this time; when I have a convenient season, I will call for you' (Acts 24:25). They are convinced that they must repent, and resolve to do it, but not yet. Young folk put it off to old age; old folk delay it till a deathbed. Every one puts it off from time to time. But, O sirs, what certainty have you of an hour, much less of a year? How many are there that never see old age? How many drop into eternity before ever they are aware?

The convinced sinner, who being awakened, says, 'What will I do to be saved?'

What Hinders Repentance?

Thoughtlessness is a great hinderance of it: 'I hearkened and heard, but they spoke not aright: no man repented him of his wickedness, saying, What have I done? Every one turned to his course, as the horse rushes into the battle' (Jer. 8:6). Men do not consider their souls' state, case, and way. They sleep away their time carelessly without due reflection; and therefore their spiritual state goes to wreck and they pine away in their iniquity, and are not aware of the same.

The love and cares of the world are great hinderances of repentance (Luke 8:14). These take up men's hearts so, as that they have neither heart nor hand for the case of their souls. How many are there, whom the world keeps in a constant hurry all their life long, that they never come to consider their way till death stare them in the face?

Prejudices against religion and seriousness are great hinderances of repentance. Some see no profit in it; but 'godliness is profitable to all things, having promise of the life that now is, and of that which is to come' (1 Tim. 4:8). Some see no pleasure in it; but 'wisdom's ways are ways of pleasantness, and all her paths are peace' (Prov. 3:17). Some think that it is needless to be at all that pains, for else will serve, but they do not consider what a holy jealous God the Lord is, and how many will seek to enter in, and will not be able.

Presumption is a great hinderance of repentance (Deut. 29:19). They hope still all shall be well, however they take their liberty in a sinful course. They abuse the mercy of God as a screen to their lusts; not remembering that he will by no means clear the guilty.

Unbelief, the not embracing of Christ, and apprehending the mercy of God in him, is likewise a great impediment in the way of repentance.

Slothfulness, whereby the business is still put off from time to time.

Obtaining Repentance

I will give directions in order to your obtaining repentance. Supposing what I have said before of the way to gain repentance by believing, I offer further these following directions.

Labour to see sin in its own colours, what an evil thing it is (Jer. 2:19). What makes us to cleave to sin, is false apprehensions we have about it. To see it in itself would be a means to make us fly from it. For this end consider:

1. The majesty of God offended by sin. Ignorance of God is the mother of impenitency (Acts 17:30).

2. The obligations we lie under to serve him, which by sin we trample upon.

3. The wrath of God that abides impenitent sinners.

4. The good things our unrepented-of sins deprive us of.

5. The many evils which are bred by our sin against the honour of God, our own and our neighbour's true interest.

Be much in the thoughts of death. Consider how short and uncertain your time is. Hopes of long life bring many into a hopeless case. And who knows when he may have outlived his day of grace, when the moment comes that God will say, 'My Spirit will not strive any more with this man, for that he also is flesh'?

Dwell on the thoughts of a judgment to come, where you will be made to give an account of yourselves.

Mediate on the sufferings of Christ.

Pray for repentance and believingly seek and long for the Lord's giving the new heart, according to his promise, 'A new heart will I give you, and a new spirit will I put within you, and I will take away the stony heart out of your flesh, and I will give you an heart of flesh' (Ezek. 36:26). 'Not for your sakes do I this, says the Lord God, be it known to you: be ashamed and confounded for your own ways, O house of Israel' (Ezek. 36:32).

What you do, *do quickly*. The sooner you begin, the easier will the work be.

Three Marks of Repentance

- Sorrow for sin, as offensive to a good and gracious God (Zech. 12: 10).
- Hatred of sin, as the most abominable thing (Rev. 2:6). This will be, (a) universal, against all known sin; (b) constant, without intermission; (c) implacable, without reconciliation; and (d) vehement, without tolerating it.
- A fixed purpose and desire of eschewing sin, and following duty; guarding against present sins, and the occasions of these we are in hazard of; honestly endeavouring after it in the use of means, and labouring to remove the hinderances to a holy life.

4

The Danger of Delaying Repentance

Yet a little sleep, a little slumber, a little folding of the hands
to sleep. So will your poverty come as one that travails, and
your want as an armed man.

Proverbs 6:10-11

I have been pressing sinners to repentance from the former text, and I hope by this time all of you may be convinced of the necessity of it. But delays in this matter kills their ten thousands. Men put off the work from time to time, till time be gone, and they are surprised into ruin, as we may learn from this text.

The sluggard's picture
We have the sluggard's picture drawn in reference to his eternal concerns; which is the main thing here aimed at. He is one that puts off his great work from time to time, 'Yet a little sleep, a little slumber, a little folding of the hands to sleep.'

In the sixth verse the slothful sinner is set to school to learn a lesson of the ant; which though she has not the advantages that he has, yet has so much natural sagacity, as to provide for winter, in the time of summer and harvest, when meat is to be got. In the ninth verse there is a rousing call to the sinner to follow that example. But behold how he entertains it; as a person that is loathe to arise, he begs 'A little more sleep, a little more slumber, a little more folding of the hands to sleep.'

Here is *something supposed*; and that is threefold:

1. The sleeper convinced that he has slept, and neglected his work. There are many who see themselves wrong, yet have no heart to endeavour to get right. They are convinced that their great work is far behind, yet have no heart to stir to set it forward.

2. The sleeper convinced that he must awake, and set to his work. Slothful sinners may see that the case they are in, is not a case they would venture to die in: they see that it is necessary to turn over a new leaf, to mind their salvation at another rate than they have done, or are doing.

3. The sleeper resolved to awake, and mind his business. He would fain sleep, but he does not design to sleep long, to sleep always. No; he designs but a little sleep, if you will believe him, and afterwards to awake; though, poor soul, he does not consider that he is sleeping within the sea-mark, and may be swallowed up before he awake out of his little sleep.

Something is expressed; and that is threefold too:

1. A delay craved: 'Yet a little sleep,' He is not thinking never to waken, never to repent, but only he cannot think on doing it as yet. However long a sleep he has taken in sin, yet he must have more. For as men, the more they sleep, the more they would sleep; so the more they continue in sin, the more they would

continue. And the more they put off repentance, they are the more unfit for it.

2. The quantity of this delay: it is but a little in the sluggard's conceit. Though the Spirit of the Lord be grieved and wearied with waiting on his awakening, yet he thinks that all is but little. If the sluggard considered that his whole time is but little in comparison of eternity, the least time he spends in his sleep would appear very great. But he considers it not.

3. The mighty concern he is in for this delay. Though his ruin be wrapped up in it, he is fond of it, his heart is set upon it; and he pleads for it, as a starving man for bread. Ease is sweet to him; and so he speaks, 'A little sleep, a little slumber.' There are three things here which he craves, each less than the other; which shows how loathe he is to bestir himself. (a) 'A little sleep;' not a dead sleep, but a moderate one. (b) If that cannot be granted, let him have but a 'little slumber;' a napping, as it were, a middle between sleeping and waking. (c) If he cannot get that, yet he would have 'A folding of the hands to sleep.' (Heb. 'to lie a-bed') Let him but lie still loitering, and embracing his sweet self, and not presently be obliged to rise to put hand to work. Love to folded hands goes deep with him.

Observe, how the hearts of sinners are glued to their sins, and carnal security. When conscience begins to draw them out of their bed of sloth, they will not yield, they will dispute every foot of ground with it. And they will take very little before they want all. O were we as nice in the point of our salvation, as in the state of blindness, in the point of our ruin, how happy might we be?

The fatal result
We have the fatal issue of this course. Delays are dangerous, but most of all in matters of eternal concern. The issue of these delays is, the man is ruined, he never awakes till it is out of time. His little sleep, spends all his little time, and throws him out quite unprovided into a long eternity.

Ruin comes upon him: Poverty and want. It is held forth under these notions, to answer to the provision the ants make for themselves. They provide for themselves in summer and harvest: so that when the winter comes, when they cannot stir out of their holes, they live on the provision they have laid in. There is a winter abiding us, a time in which no man can work, when there will be no access to God's grace and favour. Death brings in this. This time is our summer and harvest, in which matters may be secured for eternity: but the sluggard sleeps in working time; and so when it is over, he must starve and perish for ever.

How does this ruin come upon him?

1. Swiftly and speedily. So the word rendered one that travails, imports: one that walks vigorously, as a man in a haste upon the road. Though the sinner lies at ease on his bed of sloth, yet his ruin hastes on apace (2 Pet. 2:3). The sun stands not still, though the sluggard's work goes slowly on. Every breath he fetches in his spiritual sleep, draws his destruction a step nearer.

2. Silently and surprisingly; 'Your poverty will come as one that travails.' If we send one on an errand, we

will be looking for him again at the time appointed; but we know nothing of the traveller, till he come at us. So ruin comes on the delaying sinner before he is aware; destruction is at his bedside before he is awakened (Prov. 29:1).

3. Irresistibly: 'Your want will come as an armed man;' (Heb.) a man of a buckler, who may hurt you; but not you him, for his buckler defends him. Were this traveller unarmed, the danger were not so great; or were the party attacked watching, and armed too, he might possibly come off safe. But alas! the poor man is naked, and sleeping too; how then can he make his part good against his enemy? He cannot; he must fall a sacrifice to his own sloth.

What is all this owing to? 'So will your poverty come as one that travails.' It is all owing to the cursed love of ease, to sloth, to the delays and put-offs, wherewith precious time is squandered away, and the precious soul is irrecoverably lost. They delay and delay on, till the golden opportunity is lost, and they are swept away into the pit, with all their good resolutions for the time to come, which they never see.

The Road to Destruction

The delaying and putting off of repentance or salvation-work, is a soul-ruining course among gospel hearers.

Why Do Gospel Hearers Delay?

I will show why it is that gospel hearers delay and put off repentance. There is a generation that are not resolved never to repent, never to ply salvation-work; but only they are not for it yet. They hope to mend and reform afterwards, but for the present they have no heart to it: so by cheating themselves for ever. They are called by the word, and by their own consciences, to make ready for another world, to work out their salvation; but their hearts say, 'Yet a little sleep, a little slumber, a little folding of the hands to sleep;' and their practice is conformable thereto. Why is it so?

Satan lulls them to sleep
Satan has a great hand in this. If he cannot hold out the light altogether from disturbing them, he will do what he can to lull them asleep again, before they be fully wakened: 'When a strong man armed keeps his palace, his goods are in peace' (Luke 11:21). Thus he did with Felix, who, 'as Paul reasoned of righteousness, temperance, and judgment to come, trembled, and answered, Go your way for this time; when I have a convenient season, I will call for you' (Acts 24:25). When the soul begins to think on making its escape, all the art of hell will be employed to hold it fast; and it is easier to get one to put off salvation-work till afterwards, than downright to refuse it altogether. And thus Satan is always on one of the two extremes, urging either that it is too soon, or else that it is too long a-doing.

Work and worry
The cares and business of the world contribute much to this. Hence our Lord explained 'the seed which fell among thorns, to be those, who when they have heard, go forth, and are choked with cares and riches, and pleasures of this life, and bring no fruit to perfection' (Luke 8:14). How often are people in such an unsanctified throng of business, that they cannot find a convenient season for putting their salvation-work to a point? They have so many other cares upon their hands, that they jostle out the care of their souls.

They find themselves wrapped up in a cloud of cares; but think with themselves, that were they but once through that, they will ply their main work. Well, but they are no sooner out of that, than they are in to another; and so on, till the work being put off from time to time, is quite neglected. The truth is, persons in such a case will hardly find a time for that work, till they be resolute that they will take it as they can find it.

Laziness

The predominant love of carnal ease: 'The slothful hides his hand in his bosom, it grieves him to bring it again to his mouth' (Prov. 26:15). We are all naturally like Issachar, who saw 'that rest was good, and the land that it was pleasant; and bowed his shoulder to bear, and became a servant to tribute' (Gen. 49:15). Could people get sleeping to heaven on the sluggard's bed? Would drowsy wishes carry them thither? Many would be the passengers in that way. But that will not do. Men must labour, strive, and wrestle; and that is hard in the eyes of carnal men; and therefore, if it cannot be altogether refused, it is put off as long as may be. And hence never will a soul ply salvation-work in earnest, till it be effectually roused out of its lazy disposition.

Sin is sweet to them

The predominant love of sin. Why do persons stave off repentance, but because they are like those who entertaining their friends whom they have no will to part with, do therefore put off their departure from day to day? The parting with sin is like the cutting off of a member of the body (Matt. 5:30); which one will never yield to, unless he be very resolute. No man will delay a minute to throw a burning coal out of his bosom; but they will love to keep a sweet morsel under the tongue, who yet know that they must spit it out at length. And hence it is, that no purpose of reformation, which is only for afterwards, can be sincere; because it argues a love to, and loathness to part with sin.

Holiness has no appeal

A natural aversion and backwardness to holiness: 'The carnal mind is enmity against God: for it is not subject to the law of God, neither indeed can be' (Rom. 8:7). The heart will never be reconciled to the yoke of Christ, till grace make it so (Ps. 110:3). But like as the bullock unaccustomed to the yoke is loathe to steep to it, and therefore still draws aback; so will the heart of man do, till overcoming grace reach it (Jer. 31:18). Hence, when light is let into the mind, but the aversion still remains in the will, what can be expected, but that the business of repentance, which they dare not absolutely refuse, will be delayed?

They hope it will get easier

The hope of finding the work easier afterwards. The sluggard thinks with himself, that a little more sleep, a little more slumber, a little more folding of the hands to sleep, would make it easier for him to get out of his bed; though, on the contrary, the more he sleeps unseasonably, the more he would sleep; and the longer persons delay the work of repentance, it is the harder to go through with it. For sin is a disease, which, the longer it lasts, fathers the more strength, and is harder to cure. And he that is not fit to-day to repent, will be less fit tomorrow.

'There's always tomorrow'

A larger reckoning on the head of time that is to come. Hence the rich man reckoned, 'I will say to my soul, Soul, you have much goods laid up for many years; take your ease, eat, drink, and be merry.' But let us hear the judgment of God concerning this speech: 'But God said to him, You fool, this night your soul will be required of you: then whose will those things be which you have provided?' (Luke 12:19-20). God has given no man a tack of years, no, nor hours; yet everybody is ready to tell what they will do tomorrow, next month, or next year. The young people think they have a great deal of time before their hand for repentance; the old people think they have enough before them for that too: and in people's conceit there is always enough, till their time be gone quite, and they be wakened out of their dream. Hopes of long life have ruined many a soul. O to be wise! 'Go to now, you that say, today or tomorrow we will go to such a city, and continue there a year, and buy, and sell, and get gain: whereas you know not what will be on the morrow: for what is your life? It is even a vapour that appears for a little time, and then vanishes away' (James 4:13-14). But what folly is it to venture eternity on such uncertainty!

They think it easy to be saved
A fond conceit of the easiness of salvation-work. There is a generation that please themselves with the thought, that it is but to believe and repent, and that is soon done. What persons can do with a touch of their hand, they think they need to be in no haste with. But O how contrary is this to the whole strain of Scripture, and the saint's experience? 'Strait is the gate, and narrow is the way, which leads to life, and few there be that find it' (Matt. 7:14). 'Strive to enter in at the strait gate: for many, I say to you, will seek to enter in, and will not be able' (Luke 13:24). God's power toward them who believe, according to the working of his mighty

power; which he wrought in Christ, when he raised him from the dead. 'If the righteous scarcely be saved, where will the ungodly and the sinner appear?' (1 Pet. 4:18). Did men believe this, that there is such a difficulty in getting to heaven, they would not dare delay for a minute entering on the way.

Self-confidence
A conceit of sufficient ability in ourselves to turn ourselves from sin to God. That the doctrine advancing the power of natural reason and ability in spiritual things, does take so much with the world, is no wonder, since man naturally is such a stranger to his own spiritual impotency. Hence it is observed, that the first question with the awakened is, 'What will I do to be saved?' It is worth observing how the carnal heart turns itself into different shapes, to retain its sinful lusts. Sometimes the man says, that he is not able to do any good; but when his sin cannot find shelter under this covert but he is pursued hot with conviction, he puts off his reformation and repentance to another time; thereby in effect declaring that he can do it, if he had but a season for it. He that is to use his oars may row at what hour he pleases; but he that must sail by the help of the wind must set off while it blows, because he cannot command it.

Delay Leads to Ruin
Delay is directly opposite to the gospel call; which is for today, not for tomorrow: 'Today if you will hear his voice, harden not your hearts' (Heb. 3:7-8). All the calls of the gospel require present compliance, and do not allow sinners to put off till another day. It is true, salvation-work must be deliberate work; but you are not allowed a time to deliberate whether you will come to Christ and be holy or not. It is like the call to quench fire in a house, that must

presently be done, yet done deliberately, so as the work be not marred in the making. How then can it be but a soul-ruining course?

The text is very express, 'So will your poverty come as one that travails, and your want as an armed man.' And one with a thousand times more safety might venture on a sword-point, than the edge of such a divine threatening (see Prov. 23:21; Eccles. 10:18). And this threatening has been accomplished in many, whom their slothful delays have caused to perish; as in the case of Ephraim (Hosea 13:13) and of Felix (Acts 24:25). Many have been not far from the kingdom of God, who yet never came to it.

Whenever grace touches the heart, men see that it is so. Hence says the Psalmist, 'I made haste, and delayed not to keep your commandments' (Ps. 119:60). When men are in earnest to get into Christ by faith, and to get back to God by repentance, they dare linger no more in the state of wrath, they flee out of it, as one fleeing for his life (Matt. 3:7). Their eyes are opened to see their danger, and therefore they are presently determined.

Delay has a native tendency to soul-ruin, which inevitably overtakes them, if they do not at length break off all delays, and come away. This is evident, if you consider:

The state of sin is a state of wrath, where ruin must needs compass a man about on every hand: 'He that believes not the Son, will not see life; but the wrath of God abides on him' (John 3:36). To have stayed in Sodom that day it was to be burnt, was dangerous; but to abide a moment in the state of wrath, is far more dangerous. Who would venture into a house that is about to fall? Who would not presently leave it? And will men venture 'yet a little sleep, a little slumber, a little folding of the hands to sleep,' in a state of enmity with God? Surely such persons know not God's greatness, nor the worth of their own souls.

The longer you continue in sin, *your spiritual death advances* the more upon you. Every sin sets you a step farther from God, is a new bar in the way of your peace with him, strengthens your natural enmity against him, and alienates you more from the life of God. And where can this natively end, but in your soul's ruin? Are we not far enough on in that way already? Why delay more, that we may go yet farther off from God?

While you remain in this state, *there is but a step between you and death*, which you may be carried over by a delay of ever so short a time. All that is your security in this case, so far as you can see, is the brittle thread of your life, which may be broken with a touch, and then you are ruined without remedy. So that every delay, shorter or longer, of repentance, is a venturing of eternity on that uncertain life of yours, which in a moment may be taken from you.

A suicidal course

Delayers of repentance are self-destroyers, self-murderers. Well may it be said to such, 'Why will you die?' (Ezek. 18:31). Should a man wilfully neglect a remedy for his disease, which puts him in hazard of his life, he could not be guiltless of his own death; more than one who being called to rise and quench the fire in his house, and yet would lie still till it were consumed to ashes, would be blameless of its ruin. Self-love, that is, love of sinful self, is the source of the greatest cruelty; whereby lusts are spared to the destruction of the life of the soul.

By delays the interest of hell is advanced; where many are this day who had resolved to repent, but death did not wait their time, and so they were disappointed. No wonder new grounds of delay be still laid to persons' hands, for it is Satan's great drift to get men entangled in the wilderness, that they may not make forward to Canaan's land. And every new entanglement sets the soul a step nearer to destruction: and who questions but Satan has art enough to coin new pretences for delays?

No wonder Satan is most busy to ply the engine of delays, when a sinner is somewhat awakened by conviction; as he did with Felix (Acts 24:25). 'A soft answer turns away wrath' and delays will blunt the edge of convictions, as much as a peremptory refusal. Under convictions, at a sermon, or on a sick-bed, the sinner is awakened out of his sleep; but then nothing can serve Satan's purpose better, than yet a little sleep: which if they get, they sleep off the edge of convictions.

They are sinners' best friends, that give them least rest in a sinful course. And whatever men think of them now, they will think so afterwards (Prov. 5:11-13). Everybody loves ease, and therefore faithful preaching and dealing with souls, is a torment to those who love to be undisturbed in their rest in sin (Rev. 11:10). But what suits best with our sinful inclinations, is worst for our souls, and will in the end be found so. Flattery has ruined many, when plain dealing and fair warning have brought many out of the snare.

A cause for lamentation

We may lament here the case of many, no of most that hear the gospel. They put off their work from time to time, and so their spiritual case is going to wreck day by day. This is the case in natural things: 'By much slothfulness the building decays, and through idleness of the hands the house drops through' (Eccles. 10:18). They are in a dying condition, the physician comes to their bedside, and offers them a remedy; they do not absolutely refuse it, only they put off the taking of it. In the meantime their distemper increases, and death is advancing apace. The market of free grace is opened, and they are not like to stir till the market be over. O madness and folly to be lamented with tears of blood! Poor slothful creature, that is yet for a little sleep, a little slumber, a little folding of the hands to sleep, there are four things you do not know.

You do not know the worth of a precious soul, which you are throwing away for what will not profit. Will the sweet sleep in sin quit the cost of the soul's ruin? No, no: 'For what is a man profited, if he will gain the whole world, and lose his own soul? Or what will a man give in exchange for his soul?' (Matt. 16:26). Christ left the bosom of the Father, and shed his precious blood to redeem the soul. He was wise that paid the price; and if less would have done, he would not have been at needless expense of blood: he was a Father that received it; and would not have put his Son to that if it had not been necessary. Satan goes about without intermission to ruin it. But what low thoughts do you entertain of it, that will not break your rest to save it from ruin?

You do not know the excellency of precious Christ; sleep locks up your eyes that you cannot see the ravishing sight (John 1:10). The eyes of saints and angels are fixed on him, as the glory of the upper house: the eyes opened here by grace, are arrested by his overcoming glory. Hence are these rapturous expressions in Scripture: 'Whom have I in heaven but you? And there is none upon earth that I desire besides you' (Ps. 73:25). 'Because of the savour of your good ointments, your name is as ointment poured forth, therefore do the virgins love you' (Song 1:3). Zion's crowned King is making his progress through the city where you dwell; the cry to come out and behold him, reaches your ears; but while he goes by, you must have 'yet a little sleep, a little slumber, a little folding of the hands to sleep,' and so you lose the sight. The royal Bridegroom stretches forth his hand to you, to espouse you, saying, Behold me, behold me: you open your drowsy eyes, and begin to stretch forth the hand; but sleep overcomes you, your eyes close, and your hand falls down again, and the match is marred. The chariot of the covenant that is driving on to his Father's house halts at your door, and you are called out: the ship is to sail to Immanuel's land, you are called to come aboard: but 'yet a little sleep, a little slumber, a little folding of the hands to sleep,' and all is lost.

You do not know the worth of precious time. The Apostle will have time redeemed (Eph. 5:16); but you squander it away as a thing of no value; and working time is turned by you into sleeping time. Precious moments slip away, and you regard not; though once gone, they can never be recalled. What would those who are past hope, give for an hour of that time, of which you let days, months, and years slip, without any improvement for eternity? O unhappy soul, who 'know not in this your day, the things that belong to your peace'!

You do not know the weight of the wrath of God. It is true none can have a full comprehension of it: 'Who knows the power of your anger?' (Ps. 90:11). But all the elect of God get such a notion of it, as rouses them up to fly from it: 'Knowing the terror of the Lord,' says the Apostle, 'we persuade men' (2 Cor. 5:11). And if you had tolerable apprehensions of it, it would break off your sleep and slumber, and cause you to put forth your hands to work. Did you consider what a fearful thing it is to fall into the hands of the living God, and how when you fall down again into your bed of sloth, you are truly in hazard of it, it would give you such a gliff as would keep you waking.

There are three things you do not observe:

You do not observe what speed your ruin is making, while you lie at ease; how your judgment lingers not, 'and your damnation slumbers not' (2 Pet. 2:3). The avenger of blood is pursuing you, though you are not fleeing from the wrath to come. You are like a man sleeping in a leaky ship, which is drawing water every moment, and within a little it will be full, and sink to the bottom of the sea, if he do not awake and help it. Every hour your debt is growing, the cup of wrath is filling, and fills so much the faster, as you are secure.

You do not observe how near your destruction may be. You are like the old world, who 'were eating and drinking, marrying and giving in marriage, until the day that Noah entered into the ark, and did not know until the flood came, and took them all away' (Matt. 24:38-9). Your spiritual lethargy and dead sleep hinder you from hearing the sound of the feet of the approaching stroke. You lie open to the most terrible surprise, to sleep the sleep of death, which you may never awake out of till in hell (Luke 12:19-20 and 16:23). And O how sad is it for men to be past hope, before they begin to fear; to have the house falling, before they get over their bed!

You do not observe how utterly unable you are to ward off the blow when it comes, 'The sinners in Zion are afraid, fearfulness has surprised the hypocrites: Who among us will dwell with the devouring fire? Who amongst us will dwell with everlasting burnings?' (Isa. 33:14). 'Can your heart endure, or can your hands be strong in the days that I will deal with you? I the Lord have spoken it, and will do it' (Ezek. 22:14). Can worm man stand before the almighty God, whose patience may be worn out before you awake? And if mercy and patience quit the field, justice will succeed into their room; and then there will be no more sleeping, nor ease for ever.

Why Will You Die?

Why do you go on in this soul-ruining course? Have you no respect to the calls of the gospel, none to your souls, none to eternity? Why do you not do with all your might whatever your hand finds to do?

Saints

To delaying saints; for such there may be, and of such there are many at this day (Song 5:2-3); and our text is a general truth and warning. Spiritual sloth is so interwoven with our corrupt natures, that it will never be quite rooted out, till the corrupt nature be perfectly expelled. And as it remains in great measure in the saints, so it is fruitful of delays. There are these five delays incident even to the saints:

A delay of righting their case when matters are wrong, by renewing their repentance, and the actings of faith. Sometimes their case is quite out of order: their graces are not in exercise; they are strangers to the Spirit's influences, and to access to and communion with God in duties. They have a secret dissatisfaction with this, and are resolved to get to their feet again; but sloth masters them, and the work is put off from time to time; as was the case with the spouse, 'I sleep, but my heart wakes,' says she, 'it is the voice of my beloved that knocks, saying, Open to me, my sister, my love, my dove, my undefiled: for my head is filled with dew, and my locks with the drops of the night. I have put off my coat, how will I put it on? I have washed my feet, how will I defile them?' (Song 5:2-3)

The delaying to give up with some bosom-idol that mars their communion with God (Song 3:1; Ps. 66:18). They are convinced, that the harbouring of it does much harm to their souls' case, and many resolutions they have to put the knife to the throat of it, but still they draw back their hand. And from one time to another the crucifying of it is put off; so that still it lives, like a waster in the candle, causing the soul's case go to wreck.

The delaying to clear their state before the Lord. They see need to have marches rid, and to be brought to a point whether they be in Christ or not, whether in a state of grace or not. They have resolutions to put it to a solemn trial, to examine themselves, and search what evidences they have for a title to heaven: but still the heart draws back, and the trial is put off.

The delaying of some particular duty, or piece of generation-work, which they are convinced God calls them to. They have often thoughts of setting about it in earnest; but still some one thing or other intervenes, and it is put off. They begin perhaps sometimes; but it is broken off again, and they must yet have 'A little sleep, a little slumber, a little folding of the hands to sleep.'

The delaying of actual preparation for eternity; like the virgins who, 'while the bridegroom tarried, all slumbered and slept' (Matt. 25:5). They see that it is no easy thing to die; they resolve to labour to put themselves through grace into a case for it; but day after day it is delayed. The lamps are not trimmed for meeting the bridegroom. Though they be in a good state, they have not a dying frame.

To all such I would say, 'What meanest thou, O sleeper? arise, call upon your God, if so be that God will think upon you, that you perish not' (Jonah 1:6). Let me expostulate with you upon this head, O delaying saints.

Do you find yourselves any thing the nearer your purpose by all your delays? No the longer you delay, do not you find yourselves the farther from it? Does not your aversion and backwardness to duty grow upon you the more? Is not your confidence in the Lord still the more lessened? Yes; the more you give yourselves to spiritual sleep, the more you will desire to sleep.

Do not you find this the way to rank poverty and want? Your consciences will witness the truth of that, that where the diligent will abound with blessings, the idle soul will suffer hunger. Is it with you as in months past? Have you that sense and gust of religion, that access to God in duties, which you have had when you were doing with your might what your hand found to do?

Has not your poverty come upon you as one that travails? Have you not been sometimes like Samson awaked out of Delilah's lap, and found your strength gone from you when you had most to do with it? Perhaps you have spent many days in estrangement from God, with much ease; but at length some strong temptation, or piercing trial has overtaken you; and then you have sucked the bitter sap of your slothful delays.

A little more sleep, a little more slumber, a little more folding of the hands to sleep, and the occasion may be lost, the opportunity for doing neglected duties may be lost. Either they may be taken from you, or you from them. No man has a tack of his life, nor of occasions of doing good; and therefore 'as we have opportunity, let us do good to all men, especially to them who are of the household of faith' (Gal. 6:10). And though the soul that is in Christ will be saved surely, yet this will make the salvation to be so as by fire.

The long delayed work is hard work when it comes to the setting too (Song 5:5-8). When the awakening comes, there may be little time, much opposition, and less strength than otherwise you would have had, and yet more to do with it than otherwise. The longer your hand is from your case the more ravelled will it be. And it will readily occasion much fear, darkness, and perplexity in a dying hour.

Young Sinners
I would apply myself to delaying sinners, to those that are yet out of Christ, and have all to do for eternity still. They are living in a state of wrath, and yet they linger, and put off their removal from Sodom. They delay repentance, and go on in their sin. I would say to you, 'How long will you sleep, O sluggard? When will you arise out of your sleep?' (Prov. 6:9). I must expostulate with you on this head.

You young people, why do you delay repentance? Why are you like the wild asses' colts, untractable and unteachable? No doubt, you think it is too soon for you; that it may be time enough several years after this. You think repentance and seriousness suit best with the wrinkled brows, the pale face, and hollow eyes; that it is pity to spoil the bloom of youth with such work. When do you mean to repent then? It is like, it is when you are settled in the world, or when you grow old; at least the days of youth must be over first.

But, poor fool, *is the debt of sin so small upon your head*, that you must run yourself deeper in the debt of God's justice?

Do not you know that you were born a child of wrath? (Eph. 2:3); that you brought that into the world with you, that will damn you, if you repent not, and come to Christ? And will not that sink you deep enough in destruction, though you add no more to it, unless you repent?

Is not the same holy law binding on you, since you could discern between good and evil, that is binding on the oldest alive? Have the young a liberty to sin, and to cast off the fear of God and religion, more than the old? 'For as many as are of the works of the law, are under the curse: for it is written, Cursed is every one that continues not in all things which are written in the book of the law to do them' (Gal. 3:10). Here there is no exception. The follies of youth men may pass; but assure yourselves, God will not pass them: 'Rejoice, O young man, in your youth, and let your heart cheer you in the days of your youth, and walk in the ways of your heart, and in the sight of your eyes: but know that for all these things God will bring you into judgment' (Eccles. 11:9). And I doubt not, but if you saw your sinful thoughts, words, and actions, whether vain or vile, laid before you, as you must reckon for them at length, how few soever your years have been, you will see them to be more than the hairs on your heads. And I must tell you, that being yet unrenewed, and strangers to the life of grace, all your actions have been sin: 'An high look, and a proud heart, and the ploughing of the wicked, is sin' (Prov. 21:4). And is it not then time to repent?

Who has assured you, that ever you will see the age you speak of? Go to the churchyard, and you will see graves of all sizes, of your length and under. There are far more young corpses, than there are of those that carry gray hairs, ten to one. Most men and women are cut off before they come to old age. What has befallen others as young and flourishing as you, may befall you too. And therefore, since you know not but you may die young, repent while you are young, lest in the end you find yourselves miserably disappointed.

Who has best right to your youth and strength? God or the devil? God is courting you for his own gift: 'Remember now your Creator in the days of your youth' (Eccles. 12:1). Satan will labour to keep his possession. God is the first and last; and he required the first and best, the first-fruits, the first-born, the morning-sacrifice; and he requires the first of your days, and he takes pleasure therein: 'I remember you, the kindness of your youth, the love of your espousals, when you went after me in the wilderness, in a land that was not sown' (Jer. 2:2). And will you devote the first and best to sin and Satan, reserving the last and worst to your Creator?

Great is the advantage of those that get a grip of religion while they are young, beyond others, in many respects:

1. Readily their passage in the pangs of the new birth will be easier than that of others. In none is that scripture fulfilled more of the seed's springing and growing up (Mark 4:27), none knows how, than where grace joins with good education in young persons. The nail lately driven, draws easily in comparison of that which has been long rusted in. Where grace catches persons before they begin to dip into the gross pollutions of the world, it frees them of much remorse that these must occasion to those that have been led away with them.

2. Young people's affections are easiest moved; and as they move easiest, so they move most vigorously,

whatever way they be set. Hence they lie most fair for tasting the sweet of religion: 'I will allure her, and bring her into the wilderness, and speak comfortably to her' (Hosea 2:14). God sometimes dandling young converts upon the knees, and giving them sensible tastes of the pleasure of religion, is agreeable to the particular promise made for their encouragement: 'I love them that love me; and those that seek me early will find me' (Prov. 8:17).

3. They are in the fairest way to have most access to serve God in their generation. Suppose a man to be converted when he is old, his salvation will be secure; but his time for serving God's honour in the world is almost gone before he puts hand to work.

God commands you to repent presently, and therefore it is on the peril of your soul, that you venture to delay a moment longer: 'To-day if you will hear his voice, harden not your hearts' (Heb. 3:7-8). Remember that word, 'Rejoice, O young man, in your youth, and walk in the ways of your heart, and in the sight of your eyes: but know, that for all these things God will bring you into judgment. Therefore remove sorrow from your heart, and put away evil from your flesh: for childhood and youth are vanity' (Eccles. 11:9-10). A sinful youth will at length make a sad soul. You know not how soon God may be provoked against you to cut you off, if you delay. Monuments of the Lord's anger have been set up in childhood and youth, as well as in old age. Witness the children at Bethel (2 Kings 2:23-4).

Let not Satan deceive you, as if there were no pleasure in religion. No, Wisdom's 'ways are ways of pleasantness, and all her paths are peace' (Prov. 3:17). There is a sweet in religion a thousand times preferable to all the pleasures and vanities youth gads after.

Middle-aged People

You middle-aged people, why do you delay repentance? Why do not you think with yourselves seriously, where you are likely to take up your eternal lodging, and prepare for eternity by repentance? No doubt you think you have time enough too; but no time at present, for you have another thing ado, the care of a family upon your heads (Luke 14:20). When is your term-day of repentance? It is like it is when you will have more time than now, or when you grow old.

But, O sirs, *what know you that ever you will see old age?* Yea what do you know, but 'this night your soul will be required of you'? (Luke 12:20). Alas! Will men thus from time to time venture their eternal state upon a mere uncertainty? Your life is but a day, a short day, a winter day, and you have a long journey to go; your forenoon is past already, and will you sleep on till the evening that will soon be upon you? The declining sun calls you to awake.

What reason is there, that your business in the world should shuffle out your business for eternity? Remember they had as good excuses as you, who upon the sending of them were rejected, and it was declared their day of grace was past (Luke 14:18-20, 24). Oh have you not a soul to provide for, your eternal state to look after? Can you wonder, if, as you prefer the world to Christ now, he give you your portion in this life; and if ever the time come that you set yourself to repent, he deny you his grace, and bid you go to the gods you have served?

Consider the advantages you have now for seriousness, when the foam of youth has settled, and the infirmities of old age have not yet drawn on. O consider, and show yourselves men. You have spent your youth in vanity, and will you spend this age too that way? What is it you design for God, the dregs of the years, that age that is the sink of infirmities? And you will part with sin, when you can follow it no longer. O sirs, what confidence can you have, that God will accept that off your hand? 'And if you offer the blind for sacrifice, is it not evil? And if you offer the lame and sick, is it not evil? Offer it now to your governor, will he be pleased with you, or accept your person?' (Mal. 1:8).

Suppose you should live till you grow old, O how *few are there that get grace to repent when they are old?* I will not say, there are none such; but truly though they be, they are very rare. Be not you encouraged to delay, because some were called at the eleventh hour (Matt. 20:6); for if you mark the text, these were others than those that were standing there at the third, sixth, and ninth hour. We set no bounds to sovereignty; but as for those that live under the gospel, and spend their best days in sin and estrangedness from religion, common observation tells us, that it is God's ordinary way to plague them with hardness of heart, when they grow old: 'His bones are full of the sin of his youth, which will lie down with him in the dust' (Job 20:11). About three hundred years after Christ, there was one that had lived a pagan till he was an old man;

The Thief on the Cross

The thief on the cross repented at the last gasp.

His repentance was one of the miracles at Christ's death; and he glorified God more at his death than you could if you had been a penitent all your days. But though there was one that none might despair, yet there was but one that none might presume. The other thief even died as he lived. A fixed purpose and desire of eschewing sin, and following duty; guarding against present sins, and the occasions of these we are in hazard of; honestly endeavouring after it in the use of means, and labouring to remove the hinderances to a holy life.

when he told Simplicianus that he was a Christian, he would not believe him: but when the Church saw that he was really so, there was great shouting and gladness, saying, Caius Marius Victorinus is become a Christian! They wondered to see a man when he was old born again.

Will you see the deceit of delays. When you were young, did you not put it off to this time? And now when that is come, you are as unready as before. Delay no more then lest you sleep the sleep of death.

Old People

Old people, why do you delay repentance: why is not your heart bowing to God's call, when you are begun to bow to meet the grace? You that have always thought you had time enough all your days, you will think there is time enough yet. But when is your term-day for repentance? A deathbed, it is like. And when you come there, you will hope it will be but a sick-bed, and so drive off your work till the utmost point.

But, O sirs, may not *the time past of your life* suffice to have wrought the will of the flesh? Must you have 'yet a little sleep, a little slumber, a little folding of the hands to sleep'? Well, when you have taken it over the belly of God's call to you all your days, what confidence can you have to look for grace or mercy then? Sin, Satan, and the world will have all your time, and you will look to God, and seek his favour, when you can do no more. O, are you not afraid, that that be accomplished on you?

> Because I have called, and you refused, I have stretched out my hand, and no man regarded; but you have set at nought all my counsel, and would have none of my reproof: I also will laugh at your calamity, I will mock when

fear comes as desolation, and your destruction comes as a whirlwind; when distress and anguish comes upon you (Prov. 1:24-27).

If your conscience were awakened just now, you should have enough ado to fasten your feet on a promise of mercy.

How do you know, that you will get a deathbed or sick-bed? What do you know, but that in a moment you may drop into eternity, as many have done? Mind him who used to say, three words would do his turn at death. Death does not always send messengers to warn us of its approach. No, see what our Lord says expressly, 'If that evil servant will say in his heart, My Lord delays his coming. And will begin to smite his fellow-servants, and to eat and drink with the drunken: the Lord of that servant will come in a day when he looks not for him, and in an hour that he is not aware of; and will cut him asunder, and appoint him his portion with the hypocrites: there will be weeping and gnashing of teeth' (Matt. 24:48-51).

Is dying such an easy business, that you must be laying up other work, yea your main work, for a dying time? I should think, that dying itself, with the pains, throes, and sickness that ordinarily attend it, were enough of themselves. Surely, if we were rightly exercised in health, we would endeavour, that when we come to die, we should have nothing to do but die. Remember, you may come to die roving, without the exercise of your reason. But though you should have it to the last, I pray you consider, is the work of repentance such an easy work as to leave it till the time you can do nothing else? Will you put off turning to God, till you are not able to turn yourselves on a bed, but as you are lifted? Taking heaven by storm, till your strength be gone? Crying to God, till you are not able to speak two sentences at once? Making ready for death, till it come to your bed-side?

Using the Truth

I exhort you all to delay repentance and salvation-work no longer.

> Consider you do but mock God, and cheat yourselves by your delaying. For it is inconsistent with a sincere purpose to repent and turn from sin (1 Pet. 4:1-3). For he that sincerely minds to turn from sin, will presently turn from it.

> Repentance is not in your power; it is God's gift, which he gives when he will. 'God has exalted Christ with his right hand, to be a Prince and a Saviour, to give repentance to Israel' (Acts 5:31). The time of God's grace is limited: a time in which he will be found, and when not: 'Seek you the Lord while he may be found, call you upon him while he is near' (Isa. 55:6). Death certainly puts a period to it. But it seems to be clear, that men may outlive their day of grace: 'I say to you, that none of those men which were bidden, will taste of my supper' (Luke 14:24). Time was when Esau might have had the blessing, but then he despised it; but the time came when he could not have it: 'You know how that afterward when he would have inherited the blessing, he was rejected: for he found no place of repentance, though he sought it carefully with tears' (Heb. 12:17). Strike in then with the occasion; for if wind and tide fail, there can be no setting to sea.

> Though we knew certainly, that our day of grace were far from the end; yet it is a most unworthy thing so to deal with God. Shall men abuse mercy and grace because the Lord waits to be gracious? Will men abuse the divine patience, because it suffers long? What a folly is it to stand off as long as we can from him to whom we must needs submit ourselves at length?

> The time is short, the work great, and so is the opposition. Salvation-work is a great work; it is no easy thing to be a Christian; you must lay your account with all the opposition the devil, the world, and the flesh can make you; you have but an age that is an handbreadth, as nothing to do it in.

> Your life is most uncertain. We are tenants-at-will, we have not tack for tomorrow (James 4:13-14). We are agreed about the necessity of repentance; the only question is, When will it be done? God says, Today; and tomorrow is not yours, but God's. How then can you destinate for this use the time that is not yours? Return to God one day before your death, say the Jewish doctors. Wisely said; return then to-day, for it may be you will die to-morrow.

> The longer you delay, the work will be the harder. For sin becomes stronger, as the waters, the farther from the head, the greater they grow. And the arrow that going from the bow strays from the mark, how far wide will it be before it come to the utmost point? It is observed, that Christ groaned at the raising of Lazarus four days dead; but not so at the raising of the young man of Nain, or Jairus' daughter. 'Can the Ethiopian change his skin, or the leopard his spots? Then may you also do good, that are accustomed to do evil' (Jer. 13:23). Their number increases; the devil who comes alone at first, at length his name is Legion. The heart grows harder, the mind blinder, the will more perverse, the affections more carnal.

> A moment's delay may be an eternal loss, because you do not know any moment that may not be your last.

> God commands you to repent presently (Heb. 4:7). Therefore upon your peril it is, if you delay any more.

5

The Thief on the Cross
No Argument for Delay

(Two sermons preached at Ettrick in June 1717)

*And he said to Jesus, Lord, remember me when you come
into your kingdom.*
Luke 23:42

The love that sinners bear to their lusts, and the conviction men generally have of the necessity of repentance, each of them putting in for a share, do natively produce a delay. And Satan and the corrupt heart join to support the delaying tempter, both by pretended reasons, and abused examples: amongst which last none is more so than this of the thief who repented on the cross.

My great design being to convince you, that this instance can be no encouragement to delay repentance, I need not here lay for a foundation the proof of this man's sincerity, which the text and context put beyond all doubt; nor insist on explaining this his prayer, full of faith and repentance, which had a most gracious answer.

Everybody knows the story; and they that know very little of the Bible, will be found acquainted with this instance of the penitent thief on the cross; and they abuse it to their own ruin, drawing encouragement from it to put off repentance till they come to a deathbed.

We need not much wonder, that this becomes a stumbling-stone to many, on which they are ruined. Hearing the thief was converted near the last gasp, and having led a sinful life, the thread was suddenly broken, and he died happily; his day was a dark day all over, till in the evening, the sun broke out with a bright though short glimpse, and then set. That this, I say, is abused and turned to a stumbling-stone by impenitent sinners, is no great wonder, if you consider the following things.

Sinners abuse the best things

As a vicious stomach corrupts the best of meat; so impenitent sinners abuse the best things to their own ruin: so that what raises up others taught of God, is an occasion of falling to them. The altar of God, and the whole law was so to the unbelieving Jews (Rom. 11:9). Is not the very gospel, and the preachers thereof, a savour of death to some? (2 Cor. 2:16). No, Christ himself is a stumbling-block to them (1 Pet. 2:7-8).

The impenitent twist the Scriptures

There is a particular disposition in the hearts of impenitent sinners to abuse and wrest the Scriptures. Hence Peter, speaking of Paul's epistles, says, 'In them are some things hard to be understood, which they that are unlearned and unstable wrest, as they do also the other scriptures, to their own destruction' (2 Pet. 3:16). The Scripture is a light, and a rule of divine authority; and it may well be expected, that if sinners can persuade themselves of a shelter there for their sins, it will be the most effectual one. This is the most feasible means for stilling the clamours of an ill conscience, and cheating men into their own ruin.

Satan abuses Scripture to maintain his kingdom

Abused Scripture is one of the chief pieces of Satan's armour, wherewith he maintains and promotes his kingdom among those that have the Scriptures. Thus Satan said to Christ, 'If you be the Son of God, cast yourself down: for it is written, He will give his angels charge concerning you, and in their hands they will bear you up, lest at any time you dash your foot against a stone' (Matt 4:6). Hence unclean persons still their consciences with the example of David, swearers with that of Joseph by the life of Pharaoh, or Peter's. Men that are mere moralists screen themselves with that, 'He has showed you, O man, what is good; and what does the Lord require of you, but to do justly, and to love mercy, and to walk humbly with your God?' (Micah 6:8). And others satisfy themselves with good meanings and desires, because of that, 'Blessed are they which do hunger and thirst after righteousness: for they will be filled' (Matt. 5:6). Others think, they may repent at any time, from that Scripture, 'When the wicked man turns away from his wickedness that he has committed, and does that which is lawful and right, he will save his soul alive' (Ezek. 18:27). And thus it becomes harder to convince men that have some notional knowledge of the Bible, than those that never knew it.

People preserve cherished lusts

Reigning love to sin makes people very dexterous to find out shifts to preserve their lusts; as in Saul's speech to Samuel, 'They have brought them from the Amalekites: for the people spared the best of the sheep and of the oxen, to sacrifice to the Lord your God, and the rest we have utterly destroyed' (1 Sam. 15:15). What people would fain have to be true, it is easy to persuade them of: and what they are loathe to part with, it is not hard to invent shifts to hold it still. Were men willing to be the Lord's, they would be so presently; and they would be loathe to delay one moment, lest they should never see another.

To come to this particular instance in the text, I must tell you, that though here is ground of hope for poor trembling sinners, that they may be brought to repentance, and be accepted of God; yet there is no ground here for crafty delaying sinners to put off repentance, in hopes to go through with it afterwards, especially in a dying hour.

Hope for Trembling Sinners

There is ground of hope for trembling sinners. And we may learn from this instance these following lessons.

Vile wretches may become great saints

They may go long on, and far on in the way to hell, whom yet God may bring home to himself. Here is a man, a thief, whose course brought him to an ill end, to a violent death, and yet grace reaches him. See the following remarkable passage:

> Know you not that the unrighteous will not inherit the kingdom of God? Be not deceived: neither fornicators, nor idolaters, nor adulterers, nor effeminate, nor abusers of themselves with mankind, nor thieves, nor covetous, nor drunkards, nor revilers, nor extortioners, will inherit the kingdom of God. And such were some of you: but you are washed, but you are sanctified, but you are justified in the name of the Lord Jesus, and by the Spirit of our God.(1 Cor. 6:9-11)

From this it appears, that some of the Corinthian converts had been formerly the vilest of wretches, and guilty of the most enormous lewdness and impiety; and yet became famous monuments of the triumphs of sovereign efficacious grace. What a length did Manasseh and Paul go; and yet what illustrious penitents did they afterwards become? The latter justly acquired the character of the greatest of saints, and the most eminent of all the apostles.

Grace may catch unlikely candidates
Grace sometimes catches them that in appearance, and to the eyes of the world, are farthest from it. It passes by the most likely, and pitches on the most unlikely objects. While chief priests, scribes, and elders mock Christ, the thief on the cross is converted. The Lord loves to set up the trophies of his victory in the midst of the devil's kingdom. Hence is that promise, 'Behold, you will call a nation that you do not know, and nations that did not know you, will run to you, because of the Lord your God; and for the holy One of Israel; for he has glorified you' (Isa. 55:5).

Grace divides
Grace makes a vast difference between those between whom it finds none. Here are two thieves, both on the cross: grace touches the heart of the one, but passes by the other; and makes the one a convert, while the other dies hardened. So true is Paul's observation, 'So then it is not of him that wills, nor of him that runs, but of God that shows mercy' (Rom. 9:16).

While there is life there is hope
Here is one converted when near the last gasp; while his last sand was running, grace overtakes him, opens the eyes that before were closed, wins the heart that had been all along hardened. But I stay not on these things. Only the use that is to be made of this is:

Let those that seek God early be encouraged from this, that they will find him: 'I love them that love me, and those that seek me early will find me' (Prov. 8:17). Was he so ready to receive a penitent soul coming in at the last hour, then surely he will be very ready to receive you that comes in before that time. He rejected him not because he was long coming; but received him because he came. Come then forward with assured hope of your acceptance upon your early return.

Let not those whose day is almost gone, before they have begun their work, despair. Who knows but that may be done in the evening, that was neglected the whole day before? A gale for heaven may blow, that may put life in an old sinner, and make his flesh fresher than that of a child. The door of the vineyard stands open for labourers to come in even at the eleventh hour. Sovereignty is not pent up to times and ways, but takes a latitude in both.

Let us sow beside all waters, in the morning and in the evening. It depends on the working of free grace, which will prosper. We are ready to be hopeless of success, where persons have long stood out against the Lord. But God's heavy hand on a man, and a view of eternity, may afford a season in which the wild ass may be caught.

The Penitent Thief
There is no ground here for the crafty delaying sinner to put off repentance, especially till a dying hour. To set this matter in a true light, consider these following things.

A Rare Example
It is a most rare example. There is not an instance like it in all the book of God, unless it be that of Achan (Josh. 7:20-21). Yet the Lord has left that case of Achan's much under

a cloud; so that it is not positively determined as this is, though we may charitably hope the best in his case too.

What less could there have been to have cleared a possibility of acceptance, with God, for a sinner at the last, after he has spent all his days in sin? If we had not had this instance, what could have been said to show such wretched misspenders of time, that ever any that was so long a-setting off in their journey to heaven did get in? And because this says, that none should despair; must it therefore import, that they may safely delay? The sun once stood still in the days of Joshua; which says it is possible such a thing may be: but will any man delay his work in hope of such an extraordinary cast again? And why will you?

As one swallow makes not spring, so neither can this one event make a general rule that you or I may trust to. The ordinary rule is, that as men live, so they die; a holy life, a happy end; a graceless, careless life, an unhappy and miserable end. Because providence may go off the ordinary road, and do that in a few minutes with some, that ordinarily costs many years to others; can you venture eternity on that, that he will do so with you? Moses fasted forty days and nights, yet who will venture on that in hopes of having his life preserved without food? (Exod. 34:28).

Are there not eminent instances to the contrary, in which men living in their sin have been struck down in a moment, getting no time to repent of them, but fiery wrath has put an end to their days? Consider the case of Nadab and Abihu (Lev. 10:1-2), of whom it is thought they had erred through drink (Lev. 10:9); Korah, Dathan, and Abiram, (Num. 16:31), Ananias and Sapphira who died instantly with a lie in their mouth (Acts 5). But why do I instance in particular person? Did not millions die together in their sins, by the deluge that swept away the old world, with fire and brimstone that burned up Sodom, Gomorah, Admah, and Zeboim? What multitudes were there who, being warned, put off to the day they never saw? And will this one instance encourage you to delay, over the belly of the dreadful example of millions on the other hand?

The most that this so rare an example can amount to, is a possibility. It is not to so much as a probability or likelihood. That is a probable event, which though it does not always fall out, yet for the most part it does so; as that the husbandman will get more than his seed again. But from what is said it appears, that for the most part it falls out otherwise, namely, that people even die as they live. So that it is probable, that if you do not repent before, God will deny you grace to repent at the last. How then can a man that has any belief of a God, a heaven, and a hell, venture his salvation on a mere possibility, while the probability lies the other way?

Only He Repented

Though there were two thieves on the cross at that time, yet it was but one of them that got grace to repent. The one indeed was a true penitent; but the other died as he lived, hardened in his sin; no, perhaps worse, for he died blaspheming the Son of God, before whose tribunal he was to appear (v. 39). Now, upon this I would make these rational reflections:

Is it not possible that you may die blaspheming, if you do not repent now in time? You cannot deny the possibility of it, when there is such a plain instance of it in the case of one of these thieves. You think it may be you may die a penitent with the good thief and I say, it may be you may die blaspheming with the other. The one is even as certain, as to us, as the other. You live impenitent all your days; when you come to a deathbed, God may withhold his grace from you which you have all along refused; he may let you see your case hopeless for ever, and you may be filled with despair; and in that case it is more than possible that both tongue and heart may rise against God.

It is at least an equal venture, that you may die impenitent, as that you may die a penitent. You hope to repent at the last; why? because the thief on the cross repented. And I must say, that delaying repentance till then, you run the risk of dying impenitent; for the other thief died so. And who has told you, whether your lot will be with the one or with the other? Now, to repent presently, makes your salvation certain; to delay it, does at best leave it to a venture. And consider with yourself seriously, if salvation and damnation be such trifling things, as to be left to an uncertainty, you do not know how it may fall.

It is inconsistent with common sense, to leave that thing to a venture, which may be made sure, where a hit or a miss is of the utmost concern. Suppose a rebel might certainly have his life by a willing submission to his prince, should he choose to stay till he were apprehended by the officers, he would act most unreasonably, and put his life in hazard where there is no need; as in the case of Shimei (1 Kings 2:42). A thousand times more unreasonable are you in such delays of repentance, for now you may make heaven sure; but if you delay, your soul is left to a dreadful venture; and if you miss when it comes to the point, you are ruined for ever.

No but the venture is very unequal; for it is far more likely that delaying you may die impenitent, than that you may die penitent. Few took part with the good thief amongst all the crowd of spectators; the multitude went the other thief's way, mocking (v. 35).

Common observation, that tells us, that most people even die as they live. Repentance is a flower rarely seen springing up from a deathbed. A melting of heart for sin, because of the dishonour done to God by it, is seldom seen in such as have lived a graceless, careless, presumptuous life; but that disposition even hangs about them to the end.

It is certain that few are saved, in comparison of them that are left: 'Strait is the gate, and narrow is the way, which leads to life, and few there be that find it' (Matt. 7:14). As to what some say of the infants of all mankind; all that are saved must go by the strait gate, and still these are few. It is evident, that most men live impenitent; yet all must die; and therefore it follows, that few get grace to repent at their last, but most of those that live impenitent even die so too.

> 'Most...die as they live. Repentance is a flower rarely seen springing up from a deathbed.'

The sad threatenings denounced against sinners going on in their sin, with respect to their latter end:

> Because I have called, and you refused, I have stretched out my hand, and no man regarded; but you have set at nought all my counsel, and would none of my reproof: I also will laugh at your calamity, I will mock when your fear comes; when your fear comes as desolation, and your destruction comes as a whirlwind (Prov. 1:24-7).

> In your filthiness is lewdness: because I have purged you, and you were not purged, you will not be purged from your filthiness any more, till I have caused my fury to rest upon you (Ezek. 24:13).

Now, show me one promise in all the Bible, promising the grace of repentance to those that delay, for to balance this. It is true, the gospel-offer is general, and excludes none while in this world: but O what a hazard is there, that these threatenings be accomplished to the denying the grace to lay hold on them then.

Corrupt nature sticks fast in you; and it will harden you in the face of death as well as it does now, unless you get grace from above. Now, that corruption has possession long continued already, you are sure of it; but you have no certainty for the grace of God to break it in you, and work repentance in your so long impenitent heart. And therefore I must conclude the venture to be very unequal.

Repentance is not to be wrought by the sinner's being brought to an extremity, as you may possibly imagine. Here was a man that was hanging on a cross, bleeding to death in great torment, having a present prospect of eternity before him, who could have no more pleasure in the world. But did that humble him? No, no. His heart remains obdured to the last gasp. He is going into eternity; yet he is adding sin to sin, and going out of the world as he lived in it, if not worse. We find that after the chief priests, scribes, and elders had mocked and railed on Christ, it is added, that 'the thieves also which were crucified with him' joined in the railing (Matt. 27:44). Whence some think, that even the other too joined in this railing on Christ, till grace broke in upon him and overcame his nature.

The most powerful and likely means of grace will not prevail, unless accompanied with a special operation of the Spirit. This blaspheming thief was near Christ himself, and might hear his words and groans. He had the example of his companion moving him to repent. Grace was at work working wonders upon his neighbour. He had a dying preacher to call him to repent. The sun's light was eclipsed, the earth quaked, the rocks rent, the graves opened: yet for all these he died impenitent, and hard-hearted. Think on this, you that deem it so easy to repent, if you were come to your last hour.

They that delay repentance till a dying hour, readily find they have another thing to do then, than to repent; as is evident from the case of the other thief on the cross. 'And one of the malefactors which were hanged, railed on him, saying, if you be Christ save yourself and us.' Death is the destruction of nature, and therefore nature wrestles against it, though there be no hope. This man was more concerned to get his body saved than to get his soul saved. And is not this the case of the most part at that time? They have so much ado with the disease, that they can hardly get a due concern for their souls, or a composed thought.

No Evidence He Knew the Gospel Beforehand

There is no evidence that this thief had before such means of grace as you have. Who can say, that ever he heard the gospel preached by Christ or any of his disciples? It is most likely he was a rake; that if he heard any thing of God, it was from the Scribes and Pharisees at times; and may be, when he might have heard either them, or Christ and his disciples, he was about his thievish trade.

It is unreasonable to think, that it should fare at the last with those who have had means of grace all their days, and despised them, as it may do with those who never have such means till they come to die. One would think it no wonder at all, to see a man converted at his last, who gets the first notice of Christ and the way of salvation when on his deathbed. But what is that to you, who have all along been invited to repent, and come to Christ, but would not? The former is no wonder in comparison of the latter.

This conversion of the thief doubtless was a perfect surprise to him, a thing he was not looking for. But you are setting tryst with repentance at your last hours. Can you believe, that ever this thief delayed repentance in hopes of what he met with, namely, to die on a cross with Christ, and then to feel the power of his grace? Nobody can believe it. What is his example then to you? Is it rational for you to expect that favour which one has sometimes been surprised with, and got when he was not looking for it?

Not a Deathbed Conversion

This thief was converted, when by the hand of public justice he was to die. When he was made a public example to the world, and as a malefactor brought to an untimely end for his crime, he got repentance at the gallows, not on a deathbed. He was cut off perhaps in the midst of his days; at least he died not by the course of nature, nor by any sickness, but was executed for his evil deeds. And it is observable, that the one other case which looks like this in the Bible, was one of the same sort, namely Achan's.

It is evident, that wicked men who are running on in such courses as will bring them to an untimely death, by the laws of the land, such as thieves, robbers, murderers, have a fairer ground from this to delay repentance till they come to the scaffold, than you have, who are looking for a deathbed, and delay repentance till you come there. For their case is nearer akin to this than yours. But are not they most foolish if they so do, even in your eyes? No doubt they are. And so are you in the eyes of others, whose eyes God has opened.

If we compare the case of this thief put to death for his crimes, and of other malefactors so dying, with the case of men that have lived impenitently dying in their beds; though grace is alike free to both, yet, humanly speaking, there is more hope of the repentance of the former than of the latter. And this I say on these three grounds:

It is more easy to convince a malefactor upon the scaffold, of his crime, and the evil of it, and of those other sins that have been the inlets to it, than to convince another of his sin upon a deathbed, as common observation shows. Hence our Lord says, 'that the publicans and harlots go into the kingdom of God before the self-righteous Pharisees' (Matt. 21:31). Many a time is sabbath-breaking, disobedience to parents, drunkenness, neglect of the means of grace, confessed and regretted on a scaffold, while there is not one word of them from a deathbed, in cases where there is perhaps as good ground for it. When the corruption of nature breaks out in some atrocious crime that brings a person to an untimely end, there is more access to convince them of it, than others who have the same plague in them, but it has not so appeared.

The view that the thief had of eternity upon the cross, and that other malefactors have in such a case, is more certain than what impenitent sinners generally have on a deathbed. The one see they must die without peradventure, the other have some hopes of life generally while they have breath. And so the terror of death must needs be more operative in the one than the other; forasmuch as there is such a difference in the certainty of the view of it.

If we except the time in which both are actually grappling with death, the one with a violent death, the other with a natural one; the former have less hindrances from the body to prepare for death than the latter; forasmuch as the one is tossed with bodily sickness and indisposition, the other commonly is not.

Out of the Ordinary

The conversion of the thief on the cross was an extraordinary manifestation of our Lord's power, made for special reasons. And therefore though it shows what the Lord can do; it does not show what ordinarily he will do.

Consider here, to evince this, that it was done in such a juncture of time, as the like never was, and the like never will be again; namely, when the Lord of glory, the Saviour of the world, was actually hanging upon the cross, paying the ransom for the lost elect world; 'Christ being raised from the dead, dies no more; death has no more dominion over him' (Rom. 6:9).

It was a wonder wrought in a time allotted in a particular manner beyond all times, for God's working wonders. The time of the Lord's giving the law on Mount Sinai, was a time of wonders; but not comparable to this. The leading wonder there was God's making his voice to be heard, and speaking forth a holy law; and it was attended with other wonders, namely, thunders, lightnings, a thick cloud upon the mount, smoke, and fire, and the sound of a terrible trumpet waxing louder and louder (Exod. 19:16). But the leading wonder on Mount Calvary was yet greater, namely, the Son of God, and Saviour of the world, hanging, groaning, dying on a cross: and therefore the attending wonders were proportionately greater:

1. The sun was under a dreadful eclipse, for the space of not a few minutes, but three hours (Matt. 27:45). The eye of the visible world was struck blind at the sight.

2. The veil of the temple was, without hands, rent from the top to the bottom (Matt. 27:51); to show that by this death an end was put to the ceremonial law, and the way to the holiest of all made open.

3. The earth quaked at the dreadful fact of crucifying the Lord of glory (Matt. 27:51).

4. The hard rocks rent, upbraiding the spectators and guilty multitude with the hardness of their hearts (Matt. 27:51).

5. The graves were opened, and many of the dead saints arise, to show that Christ by his death had overcome the power of death over his people (Matt. 27:52).

6. The spectators of those strange things smote their breasts, being struck to the heart (Luke 23:48).

7. The centurion and his soldiers were convinced, that he whom they had crucified was the Son of God (Matt. 27:54).

Now, upon all these I would make these reflections:

Is it reasonable, because the thief was converted at the last hour, in a time that the like never was, nor will be, for you to expect that it will fare so with you? You may as well throw yourself into a burning fiery furnace, and hope to come forth safe, because Daniel and his fellows were once so delivered. Were Christ to come again, and to be crucified a second time between two malefactors, and you were one of them to be crucified with him, it might be that you might be converted at your last hour. And yet you could not be sure; for it might be your lot to be the hardened one, as it was the other thief's. But since it is not so, how dare you trust to such a late repentance?

Is it any wise strange, that amongst all these wonders of justice, power, and faithfulness, there was one wonder of mercy upon the thief on the cross? That the same power that was rending the rocks, did mercifully open the heart of one of those thieves to receive Christ and his grace? But how can you think, that the time of your departure will be a time of such wonders? And if not, how can you deceive yourself into a delay of repentance, in expectation of receiving such a signal display of divine grace and mercy?

Was it not very becoming the divine wisdom, that when the divine glory of the Son of God was veiled upon the cross, a ray of it should break forth in the conversion of one of two that were hanging there with him? That when his judges, and the rulers and people had got him on the cross as a malefactor, he should have his glory owned by one of those crucified with him: but what is that to you in a day in which it is long since Christ was set down at his Father's right hand, and his glory published through the world by the gospel?

Is it any thing strange, that when our Lord was triumphing over principalities and powers, he set up one trophy, one sign of his victory, in the field of battle? (Col. 2:15). Was it not very natural, that he who when he should be lifted up, was to draw all men after him, should actually at the time draw one after him? But what encouragement can that be to you to delay to the last, when that nick of time is over long ago? And now there are thousands of visible monuments of Christ's conquest by his death set up, so that you will never be missed, though you die as you live impenitent.

Uniquely Glorifying Christ

The penitent thief on the cross was not only sincere, but he glorified Christ more in his late repentance, than you are capable to do by thine, no more than if you had lived a penitent all your days.

When our Lord was in his lowest step of humiliation, he professed his faith of his divine nature, and his being King of the other world: 'Lord,' says he, 'remember me when you come into your kingdom.' What wonderful faith was this, that while Christ was so low as hanging on a cross, he owns him King of heaven; that dying, he was going to receive a kingdom; that he has all power there; that he is full of mercy, compassion, and faithfulness; so that the very remembrance of him would be sufficient to secure his eternal welfare! You may believe and profess all this, but never at such a time. He is now the exalted Redeemer, who has ascended far above all heavens, and sits on the right hand of God. But what is that to the glorifying of him in his lowest humiliation?

When others had crucified him as a malefactor, and were mocking him, and railing on him, as one that deserved not common compassion, he was praying to him, as Lord of the other world. If you should now do so too; yet remember how small a thing is that in comparison of what the good thief did in these circumstances.

All this he did, and more, publicly before a multitude of spectators, which you are not likely to have when you come to a deathbed. He justifies God before them all; he condemns himself; he does what he can to convince and convert his poor graceless companion, who possibly sinned with him as he did suffer; he condemns those that crucified Christ, and gives his public testimony against them, as men that feared not God.

Deathbed Repentance

To conclude this matter: Repent timeously, and trust not to a late repentance. Let not this example of the thief on the cross, or any thing else, make you to delay. Many a call you have had to return to the Lord; but to the most part they have been ineffectual. God is giving us a providential call to repentance, at this time: he is saying to us, as he did to the church of Ephesus, 'Remember therefore from whence you are fallen, and repent, and do the first works; or else I will come to you quickly, and will remove your candlestick out of its place, unless you repent' (Rev. 2:5). God knows what our present trial may end in. But in that dark dispensation we may clearly see that God is a jealous God, and makes people's sins to find them out. Repentance would be the most feasible means to extricate us out of our difficulties. If there were a spirit of prayer and mourning for the causes of the Lord's controversy with us, it would be a token for good. But, alas! the work of repentance for the most part is put off from time to time, till it be put off to a deathbed; and who can secure the tryst to be kept there?

Not the Most Useful

If it be got, it is the most unuseful repentance for God, and the most uncomfortable for one's self. Unuseful; for then men begin their work for God, when their time is ending; and so though they may be saved, yet God gets little honour from them. And uncomfortable to persons themselves; for being saved, they are saved so as by fire; they must go to heaven by the brink of hell; while they see their last sand running, and get their consciences awakened, eternity must be to them a dreadful spectacle.

Seldom Sincere

Deathbed repentance is seldom sincere. The king of terrors may make a Pharaoh say, I have sinned. But what sincerity is in the most part of those things that begin on deathbeds, may be learned from the case of many, who being past hopes of recovery from their sickness, either as to themselves or others, do yet recover, and turn just the old men and women they were before. When the best appearances of deathbed repentance are, it is hard to make sure conclusions; but as Augustine said in such a case, 'I don't say, that such a person will be damned, or that he will be saved; but you, whilst you are in health, mind the business of repentance.'

High Risk

Many trust to deathbed repentance that never see it. Some are surprised into eternity; some are tossed so with sickness that they cannot have a composed thought; some quickly lose the use of their senses and reason; and most part die as they live. Therefore repent in time, and delay no more, lest you bring the ruin on your souls that will never be recovered.

6

The Sentence of Condemnation

(Several sermons preached at Ettrick in Summer 1728)

Because sentence against an evil work is not executed speedily; therefore the heart of the sons of men is fully set in them to do evil.

Ecclesiastes 8:11

This book of Ecclesiastes is in a particular manner a book of providence, in which Solomon gives his observations upon it. It is a subject that has puzzled the best of men, how to reconcile it with the being and attributes of God: but there is no inconsistency; all odds will be made even at length.

He had observed some set on high to their ruin, made rulers of others to their own destruction, to the feeding of their own lusts, and so aggravating their own condemnation (v. 9). He had observed them live prosperously in their wickedness, die in honour, and buried magnificently (v. 10). He opens the secret of this dispensation in the text, namely, That a reprieve is no pardon. In the words we have:

God's patience towards sinners
God's patience with, and forbearance exercised towards ungodly sinners: 'Because sentence against an evil work is not executed speedily.'

It is supposed that sentence is passed in their case. There is a righteous sentence standing against an evil work, and the evil worker for what he has done: it is not overlooked, nor forgotten. (Heb. doing of the evil; by which is meant an ungodly course.) This is plain from 1 John3:8-9: 'He that commits sin, is of the devil; for the devil sins from the beginning. For this purpose the Son of God was manifested, that he might destroy the works of the devil. Whosoever is born of God does not commit sin; for his seed remains in him: and he cannot sin, because he is born of God.' See the sentence, 'Tribulation and anguish upon every soul of man that does evil' (Rom. 2:9).

The execution is often delayed; it is not speedily executed. Though the word is gone out of the mouth of the Judge, he does not presently bring on the blow; he spares the criminal a while for holy ends.

It supposes, that though the execution be slow, yet it is sure, if the sentence be not reversed, and a pardon obtained. Saying, that it is not speedily executed, he intimates that it will be executed at length.

Sinners abuse God's patience

The wretched abuse sinners make of this patience of God with them. 'Therefore the heart of the sons of men is fully set in them to do evil.' Because sentence is not executed speedily, they think it will never be executed; and so they give themselves the loose: 'Their heart is fully set in them to do evil.' They find providence gives them head, does not check and strike them down in their course: and so they even run away with themselves. Their impunity fills their heart for their sinful courses, that they drive on like a ship with a full sail before a brisk gale.

Three doctrines may be deduced from the words. I will handle each of these doctrines in order:

1. There is a sentence passed in the court of heaven, and standing, against ungodly men, evil-workers, however easy they be under it for a time.

2. The Lord oftentimes does not soon come to the execution of the sentence against ungodly men, evil-workers; but delays it for a time (ch. 7).

3. God's delay of execution is often miserably abused by sinners, to the filling of their hearts to do evil, and sinning more and more (ch. 8).

A Sentence Passed in Heaven's Court

There is a sentence passed in the court of heaven, and standing, against ungodly men, evil-workers.

They are already judged and condemned of God: 'He that believes not, is condemned already, because he has not believed in the name of the only begotten Son of God' (John 3:18). Ungodly men, evil-workers, are unbelievers; and being unbelievers, they have not the benefit of absolution by Christ: so they are under condemnation of the law for their evil works. For whom the gospel does not absolve, the law does condemn.

Only those that are in Christ, are not under condemnation; and their freedom from it is of no older date than their believing: 'There is no condemnation to them which are in Christ Jesus' (Rom. 8:1). But evil-workers are not in Christ (1 John 3:8-9). If they were in Christ, they would be new creatures; 'For if any man be in Christ, he is a new creature' (2 Cor. 5:17). Therefore they are still under condemnation.

They are in a state of death, dead in sin (Eph. 2:1). They who are morally dead in sin, being without a principle of spiritual life (Eph. 4:18), are legally dead too; they are dead men in law, under a sentence of death (John 5:24). Hence they are called children of wrath and of hell.

The power that Satan has over them proves this. They are close prisoners, bound hand and foot (Isa. 61:1). Satan is the keeper of the prison (Heb. 2:14); and they are under his power (Acts 26:18). What gives him the power over them, but that they are condemned in law? Let the sentence be reversed, and he has them no more under his power (1 Cor. 15:56).

The spirit of bondage witnesses the truth of this, convincing the sinner that he is a dead man (Rom. 7:9), and that he stands in need of a remission (Rom. 3:19). This testimony is true; for it is the testimony of the Spirit of God, whereby he brings sinners to see their need of Christ.

The Nature of the Sentence

Every evil work is a breach of God's law; and every sinful thought, word, or action is an evil work: 'Whosoever commits sin, transgresses also the law: for sin is the transgression of the law' (1 John 3: 4). No man is lord of himself but is answerable to God for every action of his life: and being guilty, if out of Christ, he is liable to vengeance, under the curse; if in Christ, he is liable to temporal strokes. So all ungodly ones, evil-workers, are liable to the curse for their sins.

The law is the accuser, that accuses the sinner of rebellion against God, and demands vengeance on him (John 5:45). Every command broken by the sinner accuses him before God; and as many breaches as he has made of it, as many articles there are of the libel against him. And though these be innumerable to men, and many of them unknown to them; they are not so to an omniscient God.

God is the judge that judges and passes the sentence against the guilty (Ps. 1:6). And he is a judge whom no artful concealment can beguile. He cannot be blinded, or biased (1 Pet. 1:17). His sentence, however severe, is always righteous (Rev. 16:7). And there lies no appeal from his tribunal; for there is none above him who is the Most High. Only, while the sinner is in this world, there is access to a remission in Christ.

The sentence is a sentence of death (Gen. 2:17); death in its full latitude, comprehending all miseries of soul and body; eternal death, in which the gnawing worm never dies, nor is the fire quenched. The sentences of men are at most the death of the body: but his sentence adjudges the soul to die eternally. The reason is, the infinite dignity of the divine Majesty offended by sin.

The Grounds

The grounds of this heavy sentence, are the transgressions of God's holy law: 'Cursed is every one that continues not in all things which are written in the book of the law to do them' (Gal. 3:10). The holy law is a transcript of the purity of the divine nature; in it he has set forth his own image. That image the sinner does what he can to deface, by violating the law: but God will magnify the law; and make it honourable, though in the destruction of the sinner. The grounds of it more particularly are:

Original sin

The sin of nature, original sin imputed (Rom. 5:12); and original sin inherent, that corrupt frame of soul that is natural to us, whereby we are prone to evil and averse to good (Gen. 6:5). By reason of this we come into the world under the sentence of death. And as serpents and vipers are objects whose destruction men seek on the first sight of them, because of their poisonous nature; so it fares with men, the very first sight of whom, in respect of their original sin, is loathsome to a holy God, and thereby they become objects fit only for destruction.

Sins of the heart

The sins of the heart (Ps. 24:4; Matt. 5:28-9) are not liable to man's judgment: but how can they escape the judgment of God, to whose all-seeing eye our hearts are just as open as our lives? He sees the rottenness that is within the whited sepulchres, and passes his sentence against lusts of covetousness, uncleanness, malice, revenge, burning within the heart, as well as against the same defiling the conversation.

Sins of the tongue

The tongue is a channel by which the heart vents much of its inbred corruption (Matt. 12:37), contempt of God (Jude 15), in his mocking, maligning, and running down seriousness, and agenting the cause of irreligion; and contempt of our neighbour, in railing, reproaching, obscenity, lying; which may show why the rich man in hell is represented as seeking water to cool his tongue.

Wicked actions

The sins of the life, wicked actions, whether impiety against God, unrighteousness against men, or intemperance against ourselves (Jude 15). None of all these will escape the judgment of God, however craftily they be managed, whatever fair colours be drawn over them: 'For God will bring every work into judgment, with every secret thing, whether it be good, or whether it be evil' (Eccles. 12:14). Sinners may forget them, and let them slip out of mind: but 'the Lord has sworn by the excellency of Jacob, Surely I will never forget any of their works' (Amos 8:7).

Omissions
Omissions of duty (Matt. 25:41). Men will find sentence passed on them by a just God, not only for the ill they have done, but for the good they were obliged to have done, but did it not. The man that hid his talent, and improved it not for his Lord, is doomed to outer darkness (Matt. 25:24, 30).

The Pronouncement
This sentence against the ungodly is openly pronounced in the word: 'But to them that are contentious, and do not obey the truth, but obey unrighteousness, indignation, and wrath; tribulation and anguish upon every soul of man that does evil' (Rom. 2:8-9). God speaks from heaven to men (Heb. 12:25); not by a voice coming through the clouds, but by his voice in the written word (2 Kings 22:19 compared with v. 11). The Bible is God's word to us, whereby he is speaking to us, and will speak to men to the end of the world, either absolution or condemnation according to their state.

It is registered there too, 'In the day that you eat thereof, you will surely die' (Gen. 2:17). 'The soul that sins, it will die' (Ezek. 18:4). The Scripture is the records of the court of heaven, where the ungodly may read their doom, and see the sentence standing against them. And that certainly is one of the causes of the neglect of the Scriptures in our day; for in it 'the wrath of God is revealed from heaven against all ungodliness, and unrighteousness of men, who hold the truth in unrighteousness' (Rom. 1:18). Ahab hated Micaiah, because he never spoke good of him. The Scripture never speaks good of a man that is wedded to his lusts, and has no will to part with his beloved liberty in the way of sin; and therefore he hates or neglects it.

It is secretly intimated by the conscience sometimes (1 John 3:20). Conscience is God's deputy within the man; and when his corruption drives him full to do an ill work, and when he has done it, to defend it; conscience will be condemning it, and him too, from the holy law (Rom. 2:15). And when it is thoroughly awakened, it will so pronounce the sentence against the man as will fill him with the greatest terror.

It will be openly pronounced before all the world at the last day: 'Then will he say also to them on the left hand, Depart from me, you cursed, into everlasting fire, prepared for the devil and his angels' (Matt. 25:41). Where it is observable, that they are declared cursed and condemned ones, before that solemn publishing of the sentence against them. For none will be condemned then, but such as are in this world before that in this life condemned already.

Howbeit, the time of the execution of the sentence, in particular, is not now intimated to the sinner. The Lord keeps that a secret, that sinners may not adventure to live a moment in the state of condemnation; but not knowing but it may be executed next moment, they may not put off a moment the suing for a remission.

How to React
The state of every ungodly person, worker of iniquity, and all unbelievers, is a miserable state, a state of condemnation. They are as really under a sentence of death, as ever any malefactor was: 'He that believes not, is condemned already; because he has not believed in the name of the only begotten Son of God' (John 3:18).

Consider the Sentence

Think on this, you young and old ungodly ones: though the sentence is not executed against you, it is passed on you; look into your Bible, and see it.

As silent as God sits in heaven, while sinners on earth are neglecting and affronting him, he is no idle spectator of their way and manner of life: 'These things have you done, and I kept silence: you thought that I was altogether such a one as yourself: but I will reprove you, and set them in order before your eyes' (Ps. 50:21). He has sentenced them, and 'sees their day is coming' (Ps. 37:13). They have their sinning day, and God sees their day of count and reckoning is coming on, in which every item will be distinctly charged on them: 'Know that for all these things God will bring you into judgment' (Eccles. 11:9). They laugh at the evil day, because they do not see it come; God laughs at them, because he sees it coming; and his will be when theirs is done (Prov. 1:26), when he will laugh at their calamity, and mock when their fear comes.

It is not strange, that the world is filled with the noise of men's lusts and ungodly lives. If you were gone into a prison filled with condemned men, you would think it melancholy indeed, but not strange to hear the iron chains rattling in every part of the room. This world is such a place, crowded with condemned people; unmortified lusts are the chains on them: and that is the reason of the grating noise which the serious godly hear from every corner. And the jailor, the devil, is going among them.

No wonder that most men love this life, so as to loathe exchanging it for another; 'But God will bring them down into the pit of destruction' (Ps. 55:23). The prison is a heavy place to the condemned man; but to go out of it is more so, for that is to go to execution (Jer. 52:11). Death brings the execution of the sentence.

Seek a Reversal

Try whether that sentence is standing against you, or whether it is reversed, and you justified.

One thing is sure, that once it was passed and standing against you: 'And were by nature the children of wrath, even as others' (Eph. 2:3). 'Cursed is every one that continues not in all things which are written in the book of the law to do them' (Gal. 3:10). 'Now we know that what things soever the law says, it says to them who are under the law; that every mouth may be stopped, and all the world may become guilty before God' (Rom. 3:19). Now, what course have you taken to get this sentence taken off? And if you have been aiming at it, have you carried it?

As your state is in this life, condemned or justified, so it will be determined at death and judgment: 'Whatsoever your hand finds to do, do it with your might; for there is no work, nor device, nor knowledge, nor wisdom in the grave where you are going' (Eccles. 9:10). Now, there is access for a remission; but when death comes there will be no more for ever.

Men are apt to mistake in this point. Many draw an absolviture from the sentence for themselves, which God will never set his seal to: 'Christ said to them, You are they which justify yourselves before men; but God knows your hearts: for that which is highly esteemed amongst men, is abomination in the sight of God' (Luke 16:15). 'He feeds on ashes: a deceived heart has turned him aside, that he cannot deliver his soul, nor say, Is there not a lie in my right hand?' (Isa. 44:20). The foolish virgins called themselves the Bridegroom's friends; but he shut the door on them as his enemies.

A mistake here is very fatal. By it men let the time of obtaining a remission slip. The oil might have been got for the lamps, if they had missed it timely. It brings a ruining surprise: dreaming of peace, they are awaked with the noise of war for ever.

Marks of absolution

They that never saw themselves in a state of condemnation, are under it to this day. For they are strangers to the very first work of the Spirit, conviction (John 16:8), 'The law is our schoolmaster, to bring us to Christ, that we might be justified by faith' (Gal. 3:24). They that have never been at the law's school, to learn that they are cursed and condemned sinners by nature, are not Christ's disciples.

They only are absolved, who laying hold on Christ in the covenant of grace have applied to the law's sentence of condemnation against them, the righteousness of Christ wrought by him, and offered to and accepted by them. Hence says the apostle, 'But what things were gain to me, those I counted loss for Christ. Yea, doubtless, and I count all things but loss, for the excellency of the knowledge of Christ Jesus my Lord: and do count them but dung that I may win Christ' (Phil. 3:7-8). They continue not in mere suspense, but renouncing self-confidence, law-confidence, and creature-confidence, have betaken themselves to him as their only refuge, casting anchor on the promise of the gospel.

If the condemning power of sin is removed, the reigning power of sin is removed too, and contrariwise: 'For sin will not have dominion over you: for you are not under the law, but under grace' (Rom. 6:14). If the condemned man has got his remission, he is taken out of his irons, and his prison, and the power of the jailor. The chains of reigning lusts rattling about you, declare you a condemned man still; but it is otherwise with the pardoned, 'There is no condemnation to them which are in Christ Jesus, who walk not after the flesh, but after the Spirit. For the law of the Spirit of life, in Christ Jesus, has made me free from the law of sin and death' (Rom. 8:1-2). If you are justified, you are washed (1 Cor. 6:9-11).

If the sentence be reversed, you will be habitually tender in your conscience with respect to temptations, sin and duty, and appearances of evil. Hence Paul could say, 'Herein do I exercise myself, to have always a conscience void of offence toward God, and toward men' (Acts 24:16). The man who under the sentence of death, has obtained a remission, will readily fear falling into the snare again. Hence we find this was Hezekiah's exercise, 'Behold, for peace I had great bitterness; but you have in love to my soul delivered it from the pit of corruption: for you have cast all my sins behind your back' (Isa. 38:17). 'What will I say? He has both spoken to me, and himself has done it: I will go softly all my years in the bitterness of my soul' (v. 15). Absolved persons may be guilty of acts of untenderness; but habitual untenderness is a black mark of condemnation.

The fruits of faith in a holy life follow the reversing of the sentence. We are justified by faith without works; but the faith that justifies, produces good works. Hence we read of purifying the heart by faith (Acts 15:9). If the curse is removed, the fruits of the Spirit will spring up in the soul, 'love, joy, peace, long-suffering, gentleness, goodness, faith, meekness, temperance' (Gal. 5:22-3). The apostle James shows that faith not to be true, that is not attended with the fruits of holiness.

Fruits of pardon

If the sentence once standing against you is reversed, then love the Lord, who freely gave you your remission, instead of leading you forth to execution; as did the woman of whom our Lord says, 'Her sins, which are many, are forgiven; for she loved much' (Luke 7:47). Remember the day when you stood self-condemned and law-condemned before the Lord, and he said, 'Deliver him from going down to the pit, I have found a ransom' (Job 33:24).

Pity and be concerned for those that are as yet under the condemnation which you are freed from (Titus 3:2-3). Where people's contempt and disdain have the heels of their pity, compassion, and concern for the welfare and recovery of sinners, it is a sad sign; speaking forth more of pride and presumption, than of themselves being in a state of remission.

Walk humbly and tenderly. The remembrance of the sentence of death sometime lying on you, may humble you while you live. It sets us ill to be proud and conceited, who owe our life to a remission. Stand aloof from the deadly snare; a pardoning God has said, 'Go, and sin no more' (John 8:11).

Bear your troubles and trials in the world patiently. Your life was forfeited, and that is safe by grace. Why does a living man complain? This is a day in which the Lord seems to be rising up to plead against the generation, bringing on common calamity. Take thankfully what falls to your share of it, in consideration that the sentence against your soul is reversed. If the seed should rot under the cold, and the beasts of the field perish under the stroke; kiss the rod, and be thankful, that the execution is not upon yourselves.

Be of a forgiving disposition: 'Be you kind one to another, tender-hearted, forgiving one another, even as God for Christ's sake has forgiven you' (Eph. 4:32). The Saviour that brought in remission of sins, binds us to love our enemies; and the bitter revengeful spirit against others speaks us unforgiven, 'If you forgive not men their trespasses, neither will your Father forgive your trespasses' (Matt. 6:15).

But if you are of those against whom the sentence still stands in the court of heaven, lay the matter to heart, and consider it as a most heavy case, as it is indeed, deserving tears of blood.

Lament

We may here lament over the case of every ungodly one, and natural man. The state of one under sentence of death, is a lamentable case. O ungodly sinner, however easy you are, God's law has condemned you, and you are under the sentence of eternal death, 'He that believes not the Son, will not see life; but the wrath of God abides on him' (John 3:36). See your heavy case in this glass.

You are forfeited of your covenant-right to the creatures, as a condemned person. Whether you have little or much in the world, it is a sorry right you have to it; a mere providential right, such as a condemned man to his meat, till the day of execution come. Therefore 'a little that a righteous man has, is better than the riches of many wicked' (Ps. 37:16). There is little satisfaction in that.

God is your enemy, befriend you who will (John 3:36). He bears a legal enmity against you, as a just judge against a condemned man. You can have no communion with him: 'Can two walk together, except they be agreed?' (Amos 3:3). All comfortable intercourse between God and your soul, is drowned in the gulf of your state of condemnation. There can be no peace between God and you. To allude to the conference between Joram and Jehu, 'And it came to pass when Joram saw Jehu, that he said, Is it peace, Jehu? And he answered, What peace, so long as the whoredoms of your mother Jezebel, and her witchcrafts are so many?' (2 Kings 9:22). How can they have peace with God, whom his law condemns? What peace you have in your consciences, God allows not (Isa. 58:21).

Nothing you do can be acceptable to God; there is a lasting cloud over your heads that never clears: 'God is angry with the wicked every day' (Ps. 7:11). While the condemning curse of the law lies on a man, it blasts all the good he does. 'To them that are defiled, and unbelieving, is nothing pure; but even their mind and conscience is defiled' (Titus 1:15).

> If one bear holy flesh in the skirt of his garment, and with his skirt do touch bread, or pottage, or wine, or oil, or any meat, will it be holy? And the priests answered and said, No. Then answered Haggai, and said, So is this people, and so is this nation before me, says the Lord; and so is every work of their hands, and that which they offer there is unclean (Hag. 2:12-14).

It mars sanctifying influences, without which there can be no fruit, 'for without me you can do nothing' (John 15:5). Hence all you do is turned to sin.

The sentence against you is confirmed daily. The truth of God confirms it: 'God is not a man, that he should lie, neither the son of man, that he should repent: has he said, and will he not do it? Or has he spoken, and will he not make it good?' (Num. 23:19). And the cords of your guilt are growing stronger and stronger; for the grounds of condemnation against you are multiplying; while none of the old debt is removed, but new is still contracted. And though one may think, that it is but dying for all; yet the punishment will be increased, as evil works are; for men will be rewarded according to their deeds.

Justice craves execution against you. There was a cry to heaven against Cain, and against Sodom: and so there is against every ungodly sinner, 'Shall I not visit them for these things? says the Lord: will not my soul be avenged on such a nation as this?' (Jer. 9:9). Mercy may suspend execution a while against the ungodly; but if they continue in that state, it cannot reverse it; since God cannot cease to be just.

All is ready for the execution. The bow is bent to let fly the arrows of wrath against you, the arrows of death (Ps. 7:12-13). The pile of fire is set on, 'For Tophet is ordained of old: yea, for the king it is prepared; he has made it deep and large: the pile thereof is fire and much wood, the breath of the Lord, like a stream of brimstone, does kindle it' (Isa. 30:33). When you lie down, you have no security, that it will not be executed before you arise.

Your life depends, as to you, only on God's long-tried patience and long-suffering, procuring your reprieve from day to day, if so you will due out your pardon. As secure as you are, the sword of justice hangs over your head, by the worn hair of long-tired patience; which if once broken, you are gone for ever.

Act Now
Wherefore bestir yourselves to get out of the state of condemnation, to get the sentence reversed.

Dead man walking
It is a sad and miserable life to live in the state of condemnation. For in effect such a life is a continued death.

It is a dishonourable life. Condemnation fixes a blot and stain on man, speaks him guilty of crimes for which he is not worthy to live. And surely the judgment of God is according to truth.

It is an uncomfortable life: 'There is no peace, says my God, to the wicked' (Isa. 57:21). There is enough in it to squeeze the sap out of all created comforts; and for the consolations of God, they can have none of them, 'Can two walk together, except they be agreed?' (Amos 3:3). The joy and comfort of a natural man is but like that of a madman; and so when he comes to himself, all is swallowed up in that, he is a condemned man. This the prodigal found, 'And when he came to himself, he said, How many hired servants of my father's have bread enough and to spare, and I perish with hunger!' (Luke 15:17).

It is an unsafe life: 'He that believes not the Son, will not see life; but the wrath of God abides on him' (John 3:36). Amidst all your mirth and jollity, the sword of justice is hanging over your head by a hair, and every moment, for all that you know, it may fall, and cleave you asunder. This our Lord threatens in the parable of the wicked servant, 'The Lord of that servant will come in a day when he looks not for him, and in an hour that he is not aware of; and will cut him asunder, and appoint him his portion with the hypocrites: there will be weeping and gnashing of teeth' (Matt. 24:50-51).

Reprieve does not come easily
The reversing of the sentence by a remission, is not so easily obtained as men are apt to imagine. Many think there is no more ado, but after a careless graceless life, when they come to die, to commend their souls to God, with a 'God

have mercy on me;' and all will be safe. But they that get out a remission, get it so as they are taught other thoughts of it. Hence is that exclamation of the church, 'Who is a God like to you, that pardons iniquity, and passes by the transgression of the remnant of his heritage? He retains not his anger for ever, because he delights in mercy' (Micah 7:18).

Sin is the greatest of evils, the deepest of all stains to wash out. Fair words, no tears, no not the blood of bulls and goats, not the blood of one's own body will wash it out; only the blood of the Son of God: 'Without shedding of blood is no remission' (Heb. 9:22); 'The blood of Jesus Christ his Son cleanses us from all sin' (1 John 1:7). Sin is the most contrary to God's nature: 'You are of purer eyes than to behold evil, and cannot look on iniquity' (Hab. 1:13). And therefore it is the object of his greatest loathing. Going on in sin, you are engaged against all the attributes of God. Sin has marred the whole frame of God's workmanship, provoking him to break it in pieces. Can it be easy to get all this buried in forgetfulness with a jealous God?

God's giving remissions, is one of his greatest works. Hence is that prayer of Moses, 'And now, I beseech you, let the power of my Lord be great, according as you have spoken. Pardon, I beseech you, the iniquity of this people, according to the greatness of your mercy, and as you have forgiven this people, from Egypt even until now' (Num. 14:17, 19). This is a work greater than the making of a world. That was done by a word spoken. But in this case, justice stands up for satisfaction, truth for the honour of a broken law, and wisdom finds a way for mercy only by the blood of Christ: 'God so loved the world, that he gave his only begotten Son, that whosoever believes in him, should not perish, but have everlasting life' (John 3:16).

Sad breakings of heart do sinners ordinarily endure, before they being once touched with a sense of sin, get the pardon of it. This was the case of Peter's hearers, 'They were pricked in their heart, and said to Peter, and to the rest of the apostles, Men and brethren, what will we do?' (Acts 2:37). Paul can tell you from his experience of the terror of the Lord; David of broken bones. However lightly you think now of the way of coming at it; a medicine given you for sweating out the poison of sin, will readily make you sick at heart, and perhaps bring you to the last gasp (Isa. 33:24).

God is pardoning today
Howbeit, God is now on a throne of grace to grant remissions: 'God is in Christ, reconciling the world to himself, not imputing their trespasses to them' (2 Cor. 5:19). You may get a pardon now in the Lord's own way: 'Let the wicked forsake his way, and the unrighteous man his thoughts: and let him return to the Lord, and he will have mercy upon him; and to our God, for he will abundantly pardon' (Isa. 55:7). Heaven's white flag of peace yet hangs out, the market of free grace stands open, an indemnity is proclaimed in the gospel: 'Be it known to you, men and brethren, that through this man is preached to you the forgiveness of sins' (Acts 13:38).

The door will close
Access to remission will not last: 'Seek you the Lord while he may be found, call you upon him while he is near' (Isa. 55:6). Abused patience will break out into fury:

> Strive to enter in at the strait gate: for many, I say to you, will seek to enter in, and will not be able. When once the master of the house is risen up, and has shut the door,

and you begin to stand without, and to knock at the door, saying, Lord, Lord, open to us; and he will answer, and say to you, I know you not whence you are (Luke 13:24-5).

Beware you sit not your day of grace, and delay not till you will find no place of repentance: 'For I say to you, that none of those men which were bidden, will taste of my supper' (Luke 14:24).

'My sins are great.'

Neither the greatest multitude, nor backsliding into them will hinder. 'Come now and let us reason together, says the Lord: though your sins be as scarlet, they will be as white as snow; though they be red like crimson, they will be as wool' (Isa. 1: 18). 'Let the wicked forsake his way, and the unrighteous man his thoughts: and let him return to the Lord, and he will have mercy upon him; and to our God, for he will abundantly pardon' (Isa. 55: 7). 'Return, you backsliding children, and I will heal your backslidings' (Jer. 3: 22). The Lord has set up instances of pardoning mercy, that none may despair; as Adam, Manasseh, Paul, and the Jews, crucifiers of Christ.

- Be sensible of your sin; of the evil of it; of the mischief done to yourselves, and the injury and dishonour done to God. Look to the law, the justice of God.
- Go to God, and confess your sins fully and freely: and condemn yourselves, acknowledging yourselves justly condemned by the law, and God to be righteous if he should execute the sentence.
- Look to Jesus Christ the propitiation held forth to you in the gospel, his unspotted righteousness offered to you, and the covert of his blood, the retiring place for safety to guilty creatures. Believe the gospel, that these are made over to you therein, and take possession thereof, by trusting wholly thereon to your remission, and the sanctification of your nature; 'God so loved the world, that he gave his only begotten Son, that whosoever believes in him, should not perish but have everlasting life' (John 3: 16). So will you be united to Christ by faith.
- Take that advice, which the servants of Benhadad offered to their master (1 Kgs. 20: 31). Put on the sackcloth of deep humiliation, ropes about your necks, acknowledging you are worthy of death, and go forth to Christ by faith; for the King of Zion is a merciful king, and will save your life.

7

Delayed Execution

The Lord often does not soon come to the execution of the sentence against ungodly men, evil-workers; but delays it for a time.

Two Methods of Providence

We will take a view of the method of providence in this matter. There is a twofold method of providence with the ungodly, evil-workers, in respect of execution against them; namely, a swift and a slow method.

Swift

The Lord sometimes takes a swift method with sinners: 'I will come near to you to judgment, and I will be a swift witness against the sorcerers' (Mal. 3:5). Sinners adventure on evil works; and God sentences them for them presently, and pursues them hard with execution, without delay.

Sometimes the sinner has an ill work in design, and the Lord counts his will for the deed, and prevents a speedy execution; as in Haman's case. He hatched the mischief, but he did not see it come forth.

Sometimes the sinner is in actual motion to the ill work, and execution is done on him before he get it performed. So it fared with the rebellious Israelites, in their attempting to go into the promised land (Num. 14:44-5). And so it fared with Jereboam, putting forth his hand to lay hold on the prophet (1 Kings 13: 4); and with Uzziah having the censer in his hand (2 Chron. 26:19).

Sometimes the execution trysts with the very doing of the ill work, so that the sinner is taken away with the stroke in his sin. Thus fared it with Nadab and Abihu offering strange fire (Lev. 10:1-2); with Zimri and Cozbi cut off in the act of uncleanness (Num. 25:8); and with Herod, who was eaten up of worms for his atheism and blasphemy (Acts 12:23).

Sometimes as the ill work is done out and ended, the execution begins. So it fared with Sennacherib's blasphemous letter. He had writ it, and was read; so his sin was completed; and that very night the Lord smote his army, and soon after himself (2 Kings 19:14, 35).

Sometimes the execution keeps pace with the ill work, and the one goes on as the other does; judgment in the several degrees following hard at the heels of the sin. So it fared with Hiel, in his building of Jericho (1 Kings 16:34).

Sometimes execution begins with the sinner's beginning to reap the fruit of his sin; when he leans upon his wall, a serpent bites him. So it fared with Ahab taking possession of Naboth's vineyard (1 Kings 21:18-19). And so it fared with the lusters in the wilderness (Ps. 78:30-31).

Sometimes when one's sin begins to work, in its bitter fruits and effects on others, it recoils on the sinner himself. So it fared with Judas the traitor (Matt. 27:3-5). It is a sport to some to do mischief to others; but before all be done, it may, in the just judgment of God, come as heavy on themselves as on their neighbour.

Slow

There is a slow method the Lord takes oftentimes with sinners (Neh. 9:17). They commit their evil works; the sentence is presently passed for them: but then the execution is delayed (Ps. 50:21). And that is what is particularly noticed in our text. Concerning this method I offer these observations:

The sinner may get his evil work contrived and accomplished, without any let in this way from heaven, by any execution against him. There is a God in heaven who has his eye upon him all along; but that God keeps silence, and lets the sinner take his swing (Ps. 50:21). He could cut him off from the purposes of his heart, and break his arm, that he should not accomplish his work: but he does it not.

The ill work being done without let, the sinner may also for a time pass unpunished, and as little notice may seem to be taken of it, as if there were not a God to judge upon the earth (Ezek. 9:9). There are times in which holy Providence, as it were, winks at ungodly sinners (Acts 17:30). Hence God is said to awake to judgment, when that time is over (Ps. 7:6).

Ill works may not only for a time escape unpunished, but undiscovered too (Hosea 12:7-8; Prov. 30:20). There are many abominations that appear with open face in the world; but there are perhaps more that are not discovered, being reserved to the judgment of the great day (1 Tim. 5:21; Rom. 2:16). An omniscient God could pull the veil off them, but in the slow method it is long a-doing.

Sinners finding it go thus, encourage themselves in evil, repeat their evils works, add sin to sin, and give themselves the loose in their sinful courses. This is observed in our text. None go to the highest pitch of wickedness all of a sudden, but by degrees. Ill works at first have a terror about them, and the sinner trembles under some fearful expectation at first: but a long-suffering God strikes not, thence the sinner gathers courage (Ps. 64:5) and ventures again, and the terror wears off by degrees.

Sinners may prosper in an ill course. So far may they be from execution done against them, that they may thrive in the world in it: 'I have seen the wicked in great power, and spreading himself like a green bay-tree' (Ps. 37:35). The sun of worldly prosperity may shine light and warm on men in a course of sin, gone away from God, and God from them. Yea, objects of God's indignation may in that respect be treated as if they were the darlings of heaven; and the objects of God's special love, as if they were the buts of his wrath: 'There is a vanity which is done upon the earth, that there be just men to whom it happens according to the work of the wicked: again, there be wicked men to whom it happens according to the work of the righteous' (Eccles. 8:14). This has been sometimes puzzling to the saints, as to Jeremiah (Jer. 12:1-2).

More than that, they may prosper by their ill works, they may enjoy the fruits of their sin, and thrive by their ill courses; as Ephraim did (Hosea 12:7-8). Riches are called the mammon of unrighteousness, because often they are got together by unrighteousness. Many a fair estate, and great worldly wealth have been got together by oppression; yea the foundation of some has been laid in blood (Hab. 2:12). A plain evidence, that men may not only prosper in, but by sin.

Sinners may get a long time of it, in which they sin, and God spares still. The old world got a long day of 120 years. Job observes, that the wicked may live, and become old, and continue prosperous too (Job 21:7; and Isa. 65:20). Sometimes God quickly cuts off men in a course of sin: but it is not always so; but men may grow gray-headed in the way of wickedness.

The Lord may seem to be in his way to execute the sentence sometimes, and yet may give another delay; his hand stretched out, he may withdraw again (Ps. 78:38). Criminals may be set on the brow of the hill, and yet be returned safe, and make a very ill use of the deliverance, turning worse on the back of it. The 120 years being out, the old world got seven days more respite, and they gave themselves the loose (see Matt. 24:38).

When execution is at length begun, it may be carried on very leisurely for a time: the drops may come very few and soft before the shower (Isa. 9:1). God may deal very gently with impenitent sinners, even when he is risen up against them, before he come to the full execution. God's judgments coming with iron hands, may yet proceed with leaden feet in slow pace.

More than all that, the execution may be entirely put off during this life. Men may live wickedly and prosperously, die peaceably, and be buried honourably; and so would wholly escape with their ill works, were it not that there is another world and an after-reckoning, and that there is no delay of execution there. This is plain: 'I saw the wicked buried, who had come and gone from the place of the holy, and they were forgotten in the city where they had so done' (Eccles. 8:10). 'There was a certain rich man, which was clothed in purple and fine linen, and fared sumptuously every day. The rich man also died, and was buried' (Luke 16:19, 22). 'There are no bands in death: but their strength is firm' (Ps. 73:4). Sometimes God makes the world witness to the execution of the sentence against an ill work: but often men get out of the world without it, in this slow method of providence.

Theological Blunders

We will account for this slow method of providence. And there is much need to do it, because there is a mystery of providence in it that is not easy to unriddle, and among men there are sad blunders about it.

It is wrested by many a sinner in his own case, to his own ruin (Prov. 1:32). We naturally have such high thoughts of the world's smiles, that we are apt to imagine God thinks highly of them too, and that he expresses his special love and kindness by them. But quite the contrary: 'As many as I love, I rebuke and chasten' (Rev. 3:19). Hence a prosperous sinner can hardly imagine himself not to be a favourite of heaven, at least cannot think God is so angry with his way as some would give out; and so he continues secure in his course (Ps. 50:21).

Being misunderstood, it is ruining to many spectators, and is in hazard of turning them atheistical, and contemners of religion: 'You have said, It is vain to serve God: and what profit is it, that we have kept his ordinance, and that we have walked mournfully before the Lord of hosts? And now we call the proud happy: yea, they that work wickedness are set up; yea, they that tempt God are even delivered' (Mal. 3:14-15). Many have no inward principle of religion and when these see that there is worldly advantage to be got by it, they embrace it, like the mixed multitude from Egypt: but when they see the way of wickedness prosperous, and sinners to keep the road for all the threatenings against them, and the godly afflicted and bowed down from all the promises to them; they are ready to think, that the threatenings and promises of the word are both but empty sounds, and that they see so.

There is a difficulty in it, that has puzzled many a great saint, and made him to stagger. So ready are we to walk by sense, not by faith. This was a knotty piece of the book of providence to Jeremiah, though he resolved to believe over the belly of sense (Jer. 12:1-2); and to Habakkuk (1:2-4). It had almost carried Asaph quite off his feet (Ps. 73).

There being a darkness on the minds of all men with respect to the methods of divine procedure, they are apt to imagine an inconsistency of this method of providence with the perfections attributed to God. And there are four divine perfections, that are apt to run a risk with poor sinners blind and rash in judging.

'The Lord Does Not See'

His omniscience, whereby he sees and notices all things done in the world, 'The eyes of the Lord are in every place, beholding the evil and the good' (Prov. 15:3). But when men themselves are conscious of their wickedness, and yet see that God does not proceed against them for it, they are apt to say, 'The Lord has forsaken the earth, and the Lord sees not' (Ezek. 9:9). So the psalmist represents men going on in their wickedness, secure as to any notice to be taken of it from heaven 'They break in pieces your people, O Lord, and afflict your heritage, they slay the widow and the stranger, and murder the fatherless. Yet they say, The Lord will not see: neither will the God of Jacob regard it' (Ps. 94:5-7). Therefore Job asserts it on that occasion, 'Why, seeing times are not hidden from the Almighty, do they that know him, not see his days?' (Job 24:1).

'God Winks at Sin'

His holiness, whereby he is pure in himself, and cannot but hate all impurity and sin in his creatures. It is certain that it is so. The angels proclaim it, 'Holy, holy, holy is the Lord of hosts' (Isa. 6:3). The psalmist pointedly declares it, 'You are not a God that has pleasure in wickedness: neither will evil dwell with you. The foolish will not stand in your sight: you hate all workers of iniquity' (Ps. 5:4-5). But when men see this method of providence with ungodly sinners, they can hardly believe it, 'These things have you done, and I kept silence: you thought that I was altogether such a one as yourself: but I will reprove you, and set them in order before your eyes' (Ps. 50:21). For, think they, if it were so, how could he bear with such unholiness in sinners affronting him, and trampling on his laws? Therefore the prophet asserts it on that very occasion, but owns a difficulty of reconciling this method of providence with it, 'You are of purer eyes than to behold evil, and cannot look on iniquity: why do you look upon them that deal treacherously, and hold your tongue when the wicked devours the man that is more righteous than he?' (Hab. 1:13).

'God Will Let Sin Go Unpunished'

His justice or righteousness, whereby he so hates sin that he cannot but punish it. It is certain it is so: 'Shall not the judge of all the earth do right?' (Gen 18:25). He has demonstrated it in the death of his own Son. But when men see ungodly sinners going on in their sin unpunished, they are apt to think, that God is not so very just in that matter, as some have given him out to be; for they cannot see sin get a just recompense. Therefore Jeremiah asserts it on that occasion: 'Righteous are thou, O Lord' (Jer. 12:1).

'God Is not Good to His People'

His goodness to his own people, whereby being good in himself, he does good to them that are good. It is certain it is so, 'O taste and see that the Lord is good: blessed is the man that trusts in him. O fear the Lord, you his saints: for there is no want to them that fear him. The young lions do lack and suffer hunger: but they that seek the Lord will not want any good thing' (Ps. 34:8-10). The prophet got it in commission, 'Say you to the righteous, that it will be well with him: for they will eat the fruit of their doings' (Isa. 3:10). But when men see this method of providence dangling ungodly sinners, and smiting the godly, they are apt to think it is not so. And therefore Asaph asserts it on that occasion, 'Truly God is good to Israel, even to such as are of a clean heart' (Ps. 73:1).

Why God Holds Back

Now, to remove these misconstructions, and account for the slow method of providence, I offer these considerations:

To Bring Sinners to Repentance

This method is taken to bring sinners to repentance, and prevent their ruin (2 Pet. 3:9); and it is becoming the perfections of a merciful God, therefore to use it.

By this means sinners have time and space to repent given them (Rev. 2:21). Were they always taken away just in the heat of their unmortified lusts, we would be ready to cry out of severity (Num. 17:12). But God gives them leave to cool ordinarily, if so they will bethink themselves, and turn to the Lord, and so prevent their own ruin.

They are invited to repentance, and drawn towards it with the softest methods (Rom. 2:4). Every sparing, preventing, bounteous mercy the impenitent meets with, calls aloud to him to repent. It says to him, 'Do yourself no harm:' it upbraids him with wilfulness for his own ruin—Why will you die? With ingratitude; is this your kindness to your friend?

By this God has the glory
God has the glory of some perfections, which otherwise would not shine forth so illustriously:

He has the glory of his long-suffering and patience: 'The Lord is long-suffering to us-ward, not willing that any should perish, but that all should come to repentance' (2 Pet. 3:9). Grave observers of the method of providence must cry out, O wonderful long-suffering of a God! The patience of the meekest man on earth, would be quite worn out with less than the half of what God bears with.

He has the glory of his universal good-will to poor sinners of mankind (2 Pet. 3:9). 'Who will have all men to be saved, and to come to the knowledge of the truth' (1 Tim. 2:4). Justice is his act, his strange act; but mercy is what he has a peculiar delight in. He is slow to anger, but ready to forgive. This is written in very legible characters in this method.

He has the glory of his overcoming goodness. To do evil for good, is devilish; to do good for good, is human: but to do good for ill is divine. Here shines forth the glory of the divine goodness, overcoming evil with good (Luke 6:35). This is goodness becoming a God!

The sinner is saved or left without excuse
As to the sinner, it issues always in one of two things: His recovery, to the saving of his soul from sin, and perishing

eternally. And God, who has a due value for immortal souls, sees that a great thing; and treats it as worth the waiting on (Luke 15:7). The Scripture holds out this as a noble attainment, 'Let him know, that he which converts the sinner from the error of his way, will save a soul from death, and hide a multitude of sins' (James 5:20). How many are there singing hallelujahs in heaven this day, by means of the slow method, that by the swift method had been roaring with the damned? 'Had I died before threescore and sixteen, I had perished, for I did not know Christ' (Turk hist. p. 96).

Or else his being left inexcusable (Rom. 1:20). The longer God has borne with, and the more kind he has been to impenitent sinners, the more inexcusable they will be; and the more will God's severity against them be justified. And so this method tends to the clearing of God's justice.

For the Sake of Future Generations
In the slow method God takes with sinners, he often has an eye to posterity.

Posterity in general
It is of use to them, whether the sinner so spared repent or not. If he repent, it is of noble use to encourage them that come after, to turn to God. How useful to many one has been the slow method which God took with Manasseh and Paul! (1 Tim. 1:16). If he repent not, and vengeance seize him at length in sight of the world, he becomes a warning piece to others that come after (Ps. 37:35-7). Though it do not, his memory rots; and the conscience of every one that notices his wickedness silent and at an end in the grave, judges him to have spent his life foolishly (Job 24:19-20). Thus many who are of no use in the world to others but for mischief, God in his providence makes good use of them.

The sinner's own posterity

To their posterity *yet unborn*. There may be vessels of mercy in the loins of vessels of wrath. Many graceless parents have been fathers and mothers of gracious children. It is for the elect's sake that the world is kept up; and if the last elect were born and brought in, the world will quickly be at an end. The law spares a condemned woman, if she is with child, till she has brought it forth: and God often spares long, condemned sinners, for the elect that may be in their loins (Matt. 24:22). There was a sentence passed against the generation which came out of Egypt, which for this very reason was about thirty-eight years before it was executed on some.

To their posterity *already born* in two ways: As Satan gives some a surfeit of religion and sobriety in their parents; so God makes reprisals on him, by giving others a horror of sin and wickedness in theirs (Ezek. 18:14). And God spares them, that they may be a glass in which their posterity may have a view of the hatefulness of sin. A wretched office, but it justifies the slow method of a holy God.

Men are often punished in their posterity. Many a poor child has smarted upon the occasion of the parent, and many a fair and flourishing family has wickedness raised. A holy just God sometimes pursues quarrels against some evil-workers through several generations, as is threatened in the second command. The third and fourth generation are mentioned, because men may live to see themselves punished in their children, grandchildren, and great-grandchildren. And they may be spared in this slow method for that very end. Witness Zedekiah.

To Discipline His Own Children

In the slow method God takes with sinners, he has an eye to his own people: 'For all things are for your sakes, that the abundant grace might through the thanksgiving of many, redound to the glory of God' (2 Cor. 4:15). As the world is kept up for the sake of God's people, so it is guided as it is by providence for their sakes. And it is their good that is designed by it: 'And we know that all things work together for good, to them that love God, to them who are the called according to his purpose' (Rom. 8:28). The way that it comes to be for their good, is by means of the sharp trial they have by it. So God takes the slow method with ungodly sinners for the trial of his own children. And it is a sharp trial to them two ways.

By the oppression of evil men
They smart sore under their wickedness. Ungodly men are God's rod, as the Assyrians were God's hand against his people (Ps. 17:14). Often they feel as much at their hand as makes them smart by the rod: 'O Lord, you have ordained them for judgment, and O mighty God, you have established them for correction' (Hab. 1:12). They always see as much of them, as occasions to them many a heavy heart, 'Why do you show me iniquity, and cause me to behold grievance? For spoiling and violence are before me: and there are that raise up strife and contention' (Hab. 1:3). Wherefore since God's people need the rod, it is preserved, and not flung into the fire.

Meanwhile this tends to their good. The ungodly oblige them to pray, watch, live in the exercise of faith, more than otherwise they would do. Hence many times the most tender Christians are found among the most profane neighbours, like Lot in Sodom, who carried not so well in the cave. For as the godly are eyesores to the wicked, so the wicked are often as whetstones and files to the godly.

By the prosperity of the ungodly

The godly smart the sorer under their own afflictions: 'Therefore his people return hither: and waters of a full cup wrung out to them' (Ps. 73:10). The prosperity of the wicked carries the afflictions of the godly to a pitch; and sometimes to a dangerous pitch, through the sleight of Satan improving it against them. This was the case of Asaph, 'Behold, these are the ungodly, who prosper in the world, they increase in riches. Verily, I have cleansed my heart in vain, and washed my hands in innocency. For all the day long have I been plagued, and chastened every morning' (Ps. 73:12-14). Job's friends acted Satan's part on that bottom, endeavouring to prove him an unsound man, because he was a man so afflicted.

But this also tends to their good. It makes them look more concernedly into their Bible, and find sweet relief where otherwise they would find no more than others do; as we see in Asaph's case, 'When I thought to know this, it was too painful for me: until I went into the sanctuary of God; then understood I their end' (Ps. 73:16-17). And it makes them to look more narrowly into their own hearts, and to their sincerity (Job 10:7). It obliges them to live more by faith, and not by sight; to the exercise of hope and patience.

To Harden Sinners

In this slow method, God often carries on his awful yet holy work of hardening sinners. There is such a work: 'Therefore has he mercy on whom he will have mercy; and whom he will, he hardens' (Rom. 9:18). And it is a most dreadful plague and judgment, whereby God ceasing to punish men for their sins one way, punishes them another way in a dreadful manner. This appears, if you consider:

It is a spiritual stroke, lighting on the soul, and therefore, more terrible than external strokes on people's bodies or substance (Rom. 1:28). Hereby the mind is blinded, the will doubly enslaved to lust, and the conscience seared: a kind of stroke rife this day.

It is a stroke, whereby the disease of sin is increased, and the gospel-remedy is rendered ineffectual. The heart being hardened, the loose is given to lusts that before were under some restraint (Eph. 4:19); and the means of grace become useless, if not noxious: the hardened heart turning the food of the soul, as it were, to poison in effect (Isa. 6:10; 2 Cor. 2:16).

It is a fearful preparative to utter destruction (Rom. 9:22). A nasty earthen vessel, that gets leave to contract more and more nastiness, and is not purged and cleansed, is, designed to be broken in pieces, and thrown away: 'In your filthiness is lewdness: because I have purged you, and you were not purged, you will not be purged from your filthiness any more, till I have caused my fury to rest upon you' (Ezek. 24:13). So it is awful. Yet it is a holy work in the hand of the Lord. God is holy in his hardening, as well as in his softening-work (Isa. 6:3 compared with v. 10).

God hardens no soft hearts, hardens none but those who first harden themselves (Rom. 1:28). Men first shut their own eyes to the light, and then a just God blinds their eyes: they are wilful in their sin, and God gives them their will (Hosea 4:17). For who can say he is obliged to strive on with them still?

Sin is a meet punishment of sin (Rom. 1:27). And therefore it is just with God to punish sin by sin, to take off the restraint from those who cannot endure it; to let them fall into the mire, and lie in it, that will needs be in it.

God in this slow method often carries on this hardening work; and that both on the sinner himself and others.

Individual hardening
In this method often the sinner himself is hardened judicially. God is at much pains with sinners to bring them back from their sinful courses; he trysts them with rebukes from his work, convictions, terrors, and anxieties, and adds to these sharp crosses and afflictions. But they struggle against all these, and over the belly of them pursue their sins: so God judicially hardens them, and carries on that fearful work in the slow method.

Denying or withdrawing his grace, and giving them up to their own lusts (Ps. 81:12). There is restraining grace given to many, who never get sanctifying grace; good motions, thoughts, and convictions are put into their hearts: these the Lord withdraws, and leaves men to the swing of their corruptions; as he did Ephraim, 'Ephraim is joined to idols: let him alone' (Hosea 4:17). They rebel against the light, and the Lord lets it die out. They are impatient of restraint, and the Lord takes it off. They like the government of their lusts, and the Lord gives them up to them.

Giving them up to Satan to be hardened by him, as the executioner of God's just vengeance (2 Cor. 4:3-4). Men resisting, grieving, and vexing the Holy Spirit of God, provoke him to depart, and to leave them in the hand of the evil spirit, who then finds easy work with them; as in Saul's case. Hereby Satan's power over them is confirmed, the opposition to his interest in them is much removed, and so his influence over them is increased.

God proceeding in the slow method with the sinner in this case, awfully carries on the hardening work upon him:

Their impunity hardens them. They venture on sin, God in anger lets them go on unpunished (Hosea 4:14). And Satan and their own corrupt hearts improve that to the encouraging and strengthening them in their sins. Thence a wind from hell rises that fills their sails. Hence in the text, 'Because sentence against an evil work is not executed speedily; therefore the heart of the sons of men is fully set in them to do evil' (Eccles. 8:11).

Their prosperity in the world hardens them: 'They are not in trouble as other men: neither are they plagued like other men. Therefore pride compasses them about as a chain: violence covers them as a garment' (Ps. 73:5-6). The hotter the sun shines, the clay becomes the harder: and the warmer the sun of worldly prosperity shines on the sinner given up to his own lusts and the power of Satan, he, like a dunghill, becomes the harder, and sends forth the more rank savour.

In the soft dealings of providence with them, objects, occasions, and means to do their ill works, are justly laid before them: they are tempted, flattered, and encouraged by others. And thus the warm influence of providence on them in external things, which should lead them to repentance, is, by means of their own lusts to which they are left, turned hardening and ruining to them: 'For the turning away of the simple will slay them, and the prosperity of fools will destroy them' (Prov. 1:32). These are to them like a full wind to a ship without ballast, in a storm.

Proper means for checking them are in the just judgment of God rendered ineffectual, and that hardens them. Thus it was with Pharaoh: the miracle of the rod turned into a serpent, waters into blood, bringing in the frogs, seemed to Pharaoh's eye-sight done by the magicians too. And thus were they rendered ineffectual to him.

The adversity and frowns of providence on the serious godly, harden them (Job 12:4-6). These are improved, by the sleight of Satan, to the contempt of both the religious and religion.

Universal hardening
In this method God carries on a hardening work upon ungodly spectators of it. Hence there is a woe to the world, because of offences (Matt. 18:7). The generality of men have so little sense of religion, and insight into the mysteries of providence, that they are apt to think that that is the best way which is the most prosperous (Prov. 19:4). Hence there was a generation that would needs make that the standard of religion:

> But we will certainly do whatsoever thing goes forth out of our own mouth, to burn incense to the queen of heaven, and to pour out drink-offerings to her, as we have done, we and our fathers, our kings and our princes, in the cities of Judah, and in the streets of Jerusalem: for then had we plenty of victuals, and were well, and saw no evil. But since we left off to burn incense to the queen of heaven, and to pour out drink-offerings to her, we have wanted all things, and have been consumed by the sword, and by the famine (Jer. 44:17-18).

And so the Lord does in his holy providence lay that method of it before worldly and carnal men, at which they, by reason of their own wilful blindness, do stumble, to their own ruin (Mal. 3:14-15).

God Is Softer on His Foes in this Life
The general method of providence in managing the world, is soft to his adversaries, and sharp to his children: 'If in this life only we have hope in Christ, we are of all men most

miserable' (1 Cor. 15:19). 'As many as I love, I rebuke and chasten'(Rev. 3:19). This is the general rule, though it admits of exceptions, both in the case of the one and the other. God's adversaries sometimes meet with sharp things, his children with soft. But the general and ordinary course of providence is soft to the former, and sharp to the latter.

He deals with us as sons

God's children are held shorter by the head, in point of particular rebukes of providence, than his adversaries are.

God sharply notices many things in his own, that he will pass in others, and greater too. Hence said Job, 'If I sin, then you mark me, and you will not acquit me from my iniquity' (Job 10:14). The common proverb holds here, 'One man had better steal a horse, than another look over the hedge.' A child of God many times pays dearer for a vain thought, than others for a vile action; for a rash word, than others for blasphemy and contrived wickedness. How did Moses smart for an unadvised word? 'They angered him also at the waters of strife, so that it went ill with Moses for their sakes: because they provoked his spirit, so that he spoke unadvisedly with his lips' (Ps. 106:32-3). Compare:

> And Moses and Aaron gathered the congregation together before the rock, and he said to them, Hear now, you rebels; must we fetch you water out of this rock? And the Lord spoke to Moses and Aaron, Because you believed me not, to sanctify me in the eyes of the children of Israel; therefore you will not bring this congregation into the land which I have given them (Num. 20:10-12).

'They set their mouth against the heavens; and their tongue walks through the earth. Therefore his people return hither; and waters of a full cup are wrung out to them' (Ps. 73:9-10).

When both meet with rebukes for an ill thing, his own often get the sharpest. Hence the lamenting church says, 'Is it nothing to you, all you that pass by? Behold and see, if there be any sorrow like my sorrow, which was brought upon me, which the Lord has afflicted in the day of his fierce anger' (Lam. 1:12). The controversy for unworthy communicating was pleaded with some godly Corinthians, to the sickening of their bodies, even to death, 'For this cause many are weak and sickly among you and many sleep' (1 Cor. 11:30).

Adversity is normal for God's people

A lot of adversity is in a peculiar manner the lot of God's people in this life, and the world smiles most on its own friends: 'These things have I spoken to you, that in me you might have peace. In the world you will have tribulation: but be of good cheer, I have overcome the world' (John 16:33). 'Therefore his people return hither; and waters of a full cup are wrung out to them' (Ps. 73:10). In the case of the church and people of God in this life, adversity seems to be the rule and ordinary course, prosperity the exception: but in the case of the men of the world, prosperity the rule, and adversity the exception.

This appears *from the Scripture*, in which we find the rod of adversity the beaten path in which the saints under the Old and New Testament have walked: the godly often groaning under the weight of their own afflictions, and the weight of prosperous wickedness in their enemies. The Cainites build cities, and have the harp and organ among them; while the church dwell still in tents: Abraham a stranger in the land of promise, while the cursed Canaanites enjoy it: Jacob's posterity in slavery in Egypt, while the Edomites were settled in their own land, having a king of their own. Perhaps among the Jews in Canaan worldly prosperity was more annexed to piety, agreeable to the dispensation they were under, in which temporal promises bear great bulk. But consider that people in comparison with other nations, and you will find their prosperity very short, in comparison with their neighbours, and their adversity very long:

> And they answered the angel of the Lord that stood among the myrtle trees, and said, We have walked through the earth, and behold, all the earth sits still, and is at rest. Then the angel of the Lord answered and said, O Lord of hosts, how long will you not have mercy on Jerusalem, and on the cities of Judah, against which you have had indignation these seventy years? (Zech. 1:11-12).

But under the New Testament the thing is most clear. Our Saviour points out this as the stated method of providence: 'But Abraham said, Son, remember that you in your life-time received your good things, and likewise Lazarus evil things: but now he is comforted and you are tormented' (Luke. 16:25; compare Luke 6:20-26).

This also appears from *experience and observation*. One needs but to open his eyes, and look about through the world, and he cannot miss to see the world's greatest favours bestowed on them who have least sense of God and religion; wickedness triumphant, while serious godliness is pressed down; sinners often laughing while saints weep.

Now, this method becomes the divine wisdom. For at this rate the evil have a taste of good, and the good a taste of evil (Luke 16:25). The former, who will at length drink deep of endless sorrow, are patiently borne with, to bring them to repentance: the latter, who will rejoice for evermore, have now the trial of a weeping time.

As a father is more concerned for, and exact in the correcting of the faults of his own children, than of his servants; so is our Father in heaven with respect to his family. The more he loves, the more he corrects with his rod: 'You only have I known of all the families of the earth: therefore I will punish you for all your iniquities' (Amos 3:2). There are some who are to dwell with him for ever: there are others who are to depart from him for ever. What wonder, that he is at more pains to purify the former than the latter!

This is most agreeable to the way he took with his own Son and his enemies. While Christ was in the world, he was a man of sorrows, and acquainted with grief; the wind blew in his face continually, till he was cruelly put to death on the cross. The axe lay at the root of the Jewish church and state, his enemies; yet was it not wielded against them all the time he was among them, nor till about forty yeas after. This was the pattern that is copied after in this method: 'For whom he did foreknow, he also did predestinate to be conformed to the image of his Son, that he might be the first-born among many brethren' (Rom. 8:29).

Delay Is Seen from a Human Perspective

Though the slow method seems strange to us short-sighted creatures, it is not at all strange being viewed in the glass of the infinite perfections of the divine nature. A thing will appear in a shallow river, that being cast into the sea will appear no more. We wonder at the slow method of providence, while we look to men; but we will cease to wonder if we look to God.

God is eternal, from everlasting to everlasting (Ps. 90:2). If men do not soon pursue their quarrels, death may snatch them away, and they can have no access more to do it: but however long the Lord delays pleading his quarrel, he can lose no time, for he is eternal.

In God's eternal duration there are no differences of time; all is present to him. Time is for measuring created beings, but not the infinite being. So a thousand years and one day are alike to him, whatever odds there are between them to us: 'For a thousand years in your sight are but as yesterday when it is past, and as a watch in the night' (Ps. 90:4). This consideration the apostle suggests, 'One day is with the Lord as a thousand years, and a thousand years as one day' (2 Pet. 3:8).

He sees exactly the time appointed for execution against every impenitent sinner, and will not let it pass beyond that, one moment: 'For the vision is yet for an appointed time, but at the end it will speak, and not lie: though it tarry, wait for it; because it will surely come, it will not tarry' (Hab. 2:3). We see the beginning and middle of things, but cannot forsee the end. God sees all at once. Well can he bear with ungodly sinners, for he sees their day coming with speed (Ps. 37:13). What needs haste in respect of God? For he sees the sinful creature is fading, and will drop down into a grave before long (Ps. 78:38-9).

He knows what he intends to do, and none can hinder: 'All the King of heaven's works are truth, and his ways judgment, and those that walk in pride he is able to abase' (Dan. 4:37). The prince that is afraid of the rebels, will strive to crush them before they gather to a head; but he that knows he can crush them when he will, may let them gather all their strength together. God can carry on the designs of his glory, by bearing long with impenitent sinners: 'For the scripture says to Pharaoh, Even for this same purpose have I raised you up, that I might show my power in you, and that my name might be declared throughout all the earth' (Rom. 9:17). Thus also he can laugh at the trial of the innocent: 'If the scourge slay suddenly, he will laugh at the trial of the innocent' (Job 9:23). Like a father holding his child in his hands over a deep pool; the child cries, and the father smiles.

He is infinitely blessed in himself; and nothing the creature can do against him can hurt him; nor in the least disturb his repose: 'If you sin, what do you against him? Or if your transgressions be multiplied, what do you to him? Your wickedness may hurt a man as you are, and your righteousness may profit the son of man' (Job 35:6, 8). If the whole creation should conspire against him, opening their mouths against the heavens, and doing to the utmost of their power against him; he might contemn their impotent malice, they would be but like men running their heads against a rock. The longest interval of time cannot make him weary: 'Have you not known? Have you not heard, that the everlasting God, the Lord, the creator of the ends of the earth, faints not, neither is weary?' (Isa. 40:28).

Both Swift and Slow Judgements Are Necessary

There is a necessity for both the swift and slow methods being used by providence in the government of the world; it is so corrupt and atheistical.

The swift method is necessary to show, that there is a God to judge upon the earth: 'The righteous will rejoice when he sees the vengeance: he will wash his feet in the blood of the wicked. So that a man will say, Verily there is a reward for the righteous: verily he is God that judges in the earth' (Ps. 58:10-11). For as ordinary as the slow method is, there are never wanting instances now and then of swift process against ungodly sinners: which is necessary to bear testimony to the being of a God, and of a providence concerned in human affairs. And there are as many of these, as may give sufficient warning to all.

The slow method is necessary, to show there is a judgment to come:

> We ourselves glory in you in the churches of God, for your patience and faith in all your persecutions and tribulations that you endure. Which is a manifest token of the righteous judgment of God, that you may be counted worthy of the kingdom of God to recompense tribulation to them that trouble you; and to you who are troubled, rest with us: when the Lord Jesus will be revealed from heaven, with his almighty angels (2 Thess. 1:4-7).

What the carnal world improves in behalf of atheism, is necessary to prevent Sadduceism: for if all men's wickedness were punished in this life, it would thence be concluded, that there were no after-reckoning: but there is never a sentence passed against an evil work, that is missed to be executed now, but is a pledge of the judgment to come.

The Slowest Vengeance Will Be the Surest

The slowest vengeance against impenitent sinners will be sure vengeance; and the slower it is in coming, it will be the sorer when it comes: 'To me belongs vengeance, and recompense; their foot will slide in due time: for the day of their calamity is at hand, and the things that will come upon them make haste' (Deut. 32:35). The old world was spared 120 years, but was swept away at length.

Let sinners be spared never so long, not one of all their ill works will, or can be forgotten. They may have forgot them themselves, but God never will. There is a book of remembrance of their ill, as well as of the saints' good words and works: 'The Lord has sworn by the excellency of Jacob, Surely I will never forget any of their works' (Amos 8:7). 'These things have you done, and I kept silence: you thought that I was altogether such a one as yourself: but I will reprove you, and set them in order before your eyes' (Ps. 50:21).

The longer sinners are spared, their counts will be the greater, and all will come on at once (Luke 11:50; 1 Sam. 3:12). It is people's mercy, that God ceases not to be a reprover to them; as it is the mercy of weak people to pay their debt by littles, whereas they are broken if it get leave to run on.

When it comes on the impenitent sinner, God will charge both the interest and the principal sum together. They will not only pay for their ill works, but for their mercies, and the sparing they have gotten: 'Or do you despise the riches of his goodness, and forbearance, and long-suffering; not knowing that the goodness of God leads you to repentance? But after your hardness and impenitent heart, you are treasuring up for yourself wrath in the day of wrath, and revelation of the righteous judgment of God' (Rom. 2:4-5). What aggravated their sin, will aggravate their condemnation and punishment.

And however long the execution of the sentence against ungodly sinners, evil-workers, may be delayed, and how many external favours of providence be heaped on them; all will appear but small and short, when one considers the severity of the execution when it comes. They will at length be cut asunder (Matt. 24:51). In flaming fire he will take vengeance on them (2 Thess. 1:8). They will fall into the hands of the living God.

Consider the eternity of it. That is a killing aggravation in the sentence, Depart into everlasting fire. If the worm were once awakened, and set on them, it dies not; the fire once kindled, will not be quenched.

Using the Truth

> That present ease and prosperity in the world are not a sure sign of God's special favour (Eccles. 9:1-2). Indeed men are apt to construe it so; and Satan and the deceitful heart help them to draw such a conclusion. But so far is it from being such a sign, that it may very well consist with their being in a state of wrath, under a sentence of condemnation; and is so with many.

> That present ease, impunity, and prosperity, are no security against the time to come. Men are ready to be secure upon it, and to dream that to-morrow will be as this day: 'He has said in his heart, I will not be moved: for I will never be in adversity' (Ps. 10:6). But the mountain may be standing sure now, that before long may be overturned. The sun shined fair on Sodom, the morning of that day in which God rained fire and brimstone on it. The rich man was full of thoughts of ease in that day, in the night of which he was struck (Luke 12:18-20).

> There cannot be such worth in outward prosperity, nor such evil in affliction, as we generally imagine. For a holy, wise God would never heap what is really best on the objects of his wrath, and what is really worst on the objects of his love. Were there as much real value in the world's wealth, ease, and honour, health, strength, silver, gold, as we imagine; or were there as much evil in trouble, adversity, as we think, would they be so dealt, as that the greatest share of the former should be given to the condemned, and of the latter to the justified? It is owing to the weakness of human sight, that so much beauty appears in some human faces, and in some victuals we feed on. If they were looked at with a microscope, the beauty would disappear. Faith is the microscope here (Eccles. 1:2; 2 Cor. 4:17-18).

> God is a patient and long-suffering God, not subject to passions as we are (2 Pet. 3:9). If he were liable to the transports of passion as we are, the world would have been many times burnt to ashes before now; considering the provocations given to the eyes of his glory. But infinite mind enjoys the profoundest serenity and calm, beholding all the confusions of evil-workers in the world.

> Sad and heavy strokes may be abiding a land and generation, though long warded off. Long has the Lord borne with this apostatising generation in principle and practice; and long have we been threatened: and through the delay, we have been brought to say, 'The days are prolonged, and every vision fails' (Ezek. 12:22). But a reprieve is no pardon; the cloud is still hanging over our heads, and it is to be feared, that some will live to see a fearful breaking of it.

> Let ungodly sinners be exhorted to repent of their evil works, and beware of abusing the divine patience with them. You have heard the slow method rationally accounted for. If hereafter you will deceive yourselves in sin from your impunity and prosperity; know, that you are wilfully blind, that you will be inexcusable, and your blood will be on your heads.

>> But let the sense of gratitude move you to repentance (Rom. 2:4). Think with yourselves, what case you had been in, if God had struck you down, as he could, in the very act of your evil work; how you might have been beyond all hope and possibility of recovery. You owe your life to the slow method of providence; his patience exercised towards you has kept your soul back from the pit. Therefore repent, and go no farther on.

>> Let the account you have heard of the slow method, frighten you from abusing it. I am sure, you cannot but see now, that there is no ground to take encouragement to sin from it. Consider what has been said, and show yourselves men. If you go on to abuse it so, you make a jest of a most serious and wise dispensation of providence. You turn your food into poison, and stumble at noonday. And it will be a sure presage of everlasting ruin to you: 'Who is wise, and he will understand these things? Prudent, and he will know them? For the ways of the Lord are right, and the just will walk in them: but the transgressors will fall therein' (Hosea 14:9).

> Let all beware of censuring the slow method of providence with ungodly sinners, evil workers. Take heed how you speak on that head; beware of risings of the corrupt heart upon it. For however rationally you think you pronounce upon the matter, sooner or later you will be made to recant that sentence, either in mercy, as Job did (42:3), and as Asaph did (Ps. 73:22), or in wrath (Mal. 3:14-15, 18).

> > Consider there may be a mystery in the dispensations of providence; but there can be no iniquity, error, or mistake: 'He is the rock, his work is perfect: for all his ways are judgment: a God of truth, and without iniquity, just and right is he' (Deut. 32:4). Silently adore that wisdom and the deep design of providence which you cannot see through, that certainly are in the slow method God uses with some ungodly sinners, evil-workers. Though you cannot see how God's glory can miss to suffer by it, believe that God will doubtless get glory by it.

> > The mystery of that dispensation in the case of every ungodly sinner, will be opened out before the world at length, to the satisfaction of all humble waiters; and the confusion of the impenitent evil-workers, scoffers, and murmurers: 'Judge nothing before the time, until the Lord come, who both will bring to light the hidden things of darkness, and will make manifest the counsels of the hearts: and then will every man have praise of God' (1 Cor. 4:5). Be not rash, wait the end, and then you will be allowed to judge: 'He that answers a matter before he hears it, it is folly and shame to him' (Prov. 18:13). But why should you judge of the web of providence before it be wrought out?

> Fret not at, neither envy prosperous wickedness: 'Let not your heart envy sinners: but be you in the fear of the Lord all the day long' (Prov. 23:17). 'Fret not yourself because of evil-doers, neither be you envious against the workers of iniquity' (Ps. 37:1). Who would envy the state of a condemned man, though he have a long reprieve, and enjoy many comforts in the iron house? Such is the case of the ungodly, whatever world's ease they have. And therefore they are just objects of pity and compassion, but not of envy. One had better be a pardoned one in the depth of worldly misery, than in a state of wrath and condemnation in the top of worldly felicity, 'For what is a man profited, if he will gain the whole world, and lose his own soul? Or what will a man give in exchange for his soul?' (Matt. 16:26).

>> Consider such fretting and envy proceeds from a distempered heart: 'So foolish was I, and ignorant: I was as a beast before you' (Ps. 73:22). It is the produce of a mixture of ignorance, rashness and inconsideration, unbelief and worldly-mindedness. And there needs only to cure it, to have our eyes opened, to see things in their true state; the laying aside of unruly passions; faith and due weanedness from the world: 'Fret not yourself because of evil-doers, neither be envious against the workers of iniquity. For they will soon be cut down like the grass, and wither as the green herb' (Ps. 37:1-2).

>> Every one's state is to be rated, according as it is before God. If God be one's friend, he is a happy man, though the world should never give him its word nor kind look. If God is one's enemy, he is a miserable man, though all the men and things of the world should favour him to his wish. For as is one's state with God, so is his present safety; and so will be his well or woe through eternity.

> Let all learn to regulate their conduct by the example of God in this his government of the world, so far as it is proposed for our imitation: 'Be you therefore followers of God as dear children' (Eph. 5:1).

>> And we may learn from it to be patient and slow to anger. How ill it becomes us to be ready to fire at every provocation, against our fellow-creatures; when the highest One uses so much patience towards us? (Matt. 18:23). The more meekly and patiently one carries himself, he is the more like to God, who has set us an example.

>> Learn to bear with sinners, in order to the seeking of their recovery: 'Brethren, if a man be overtaken in a fault, you which are spiritual, restore such an one in the Spirit of meekness; considering yourself, lest you also be tempted' (Gal. 6:1). Not that we are to suffer sin upon him, so far as it is in our power to remove it. God can bring good out of evil, but we cannot do that: therefore that part of the conduct of providence towards the ungodly, we are not called to imitate. But let us be followers of God, in dealing still with the worst of sinners to recover them, and not give them over for hopeless.

>> To do good to the worthless, unthankful, and evil: 'Love you your enemies, and do good, and lend, hoping for nothing again: and your reward will be great, and you will be the children of the Highest: for he is kind to the unthankful, and to the evil' (Luke 6:35). It is a naughty world, that people had need of such a principle to prompt them to do good to others. If we confine our good to those that do good to us, what do we more than others? If we confine it to those worthy of it, we do it only for the creature's sake. But if we propose to follow the example of God, we will do good to all as we have access, and act from a Christian principle in it.

> Let us not be secure with respect to the case of the land and generation we live in. Let us not think that God has forgotten the iniquity of our fathers in their perfidy and cruelty against the godly for his cause; or that he approves of the course of apostacy from the truth and holiness of the gospel this day, whereby the present generation has entered itself heir to the apostatising, persecuting generation that went before. The sentence is not executed, yet it is but delayed; therefore we may look for it, if repentance prevent it not.

233

8

God's Patience Abused

God's patience in the delay of execution is often miserably abused by sinners, to the filling of their hearts to do evil, and sinning more and more.

How Sinners Abuse the Delay

They abuse it to carnal security: 'He has said in his heart, I will not be moved: for I will never be in adversity' (Ps. 10:6). Finding that God does not execute his threatenings against them, they conclude they are in no hazard: and they begin to look on them as mere scarecrows, 'His ways are always grievous; your judgments are far above out of his sight' (Ps. 10:5). And so they go on securely in their ungodly courses. Hence it is that the execution overtakes them quite unexpectedly: 'The day of the Lord so comes as a thief in the night. For when they will say, Peace and safety; then sudden destruction comes upon them, as travail upon a woman with child; and they will not escape' (1 Thess. 5:2-3).

They abuse it to a sensual life, in which their aim is not to keep a clean conscience, but to gratify their senses, as their circumstances in the world will permit; as the rich man did, 'I will say to my soul, Soul, you have much goods laid up for many years; take your ease, eat, drink and be merry' (Luke 12:19). So the more that providence favours them in external things, the more sensual they are, fulfilling the desires of the flesh and of the mind: 'According to their pasture, so were they filled: they were filled, and their heart was exalted; therefore have they forgotten me' (Hosea 13:6). Hence the lives of many are trifled away, and wholly spent in making provision for the flesh, 'the lust of the flesh, the lust of the eyes, and the pride of life.' And that is endless business: 'All things are full of labour, man cannot utter it: the eye is not satisfied with seeing, nor the ear filled with hearing' (Eccles. 1:8).

They abuse it to impudence in sin (Jer. 6:14-15). When God strikes men in a sinful course, they are ashamed readily as pointed at by the hand of heaven, as transgressors: but when men prosper in a sinful course, they put on a brow of brass, they father a stock of impudence in sin, as if providence had given them a patent for wickedness: 'They are not in trouble as other men: neither are they plagued like other men. Therefore pride compasses them about as a chain: violence covers them as a garment' (Ps. 73:5-6).

They abuse it to contempt of God, and all that is sacred: 'They set their mouth against the heavens; and their tongue walks through the earth' (Ps. 73:9). Agur saw the danger of this snare, and therefore prayed thus, 'Remove far from me vanity and lies; give me neither poverty, nor riches, feed me with food convenient for me: lest I be full, and deny you, and say, Who is the Lord? Or lest I be poor, and steal, and take the name of my God in vain' (Prov. 30:8-9). Israel fell into it: 'Jeshurun waxed fat, and kicked: you are waxed fat, you are grown thick, you are covered with fatness; then he forsook God which made him, and lightly esteemed the

Rock of his salvation' (Deut. 32:15). The ungodly have not love to God: if they have any thing that way of such affections, it is fear of him, a slavish fear of his wrath, springing from the love of themselves: this fear they lose also, when God delays to strike. And so it issues in contempt, as is natural in the case of one we neither love nor fear. And then all that is sacred is despised.

They abuse it to sinning more diffusely, giving loose reins to their several lusts (Jer. 7:9-10). One sin makes way for another, and prosperity in a sinful course gives many occasions of sin: and as the vicious stomach, the more it receives, breeds the more ill humours; so the more one prospers in a sinful course, the more vile does he grow.

They abuse it to sinning more eagerly: 'Being past feeling, they have given themselves over to lasciviousness, to work all uncleanness with greediness' (Eph. 4:19). The more that lusts are fed, the more strong they grow, and carry out the man more violently to satisfy them. So that the heart in that case is like a ship having a full gale of wind, and is eagerly set to do evil.

They abuse it to incorrigibleness and obstinacy in sin (Jer. 22:21). A prosperous sinner quickly gets above reproofs (Hosea 4:4). As affliction tends to humble, prosperity puffs up an ungracious heart: and the heart swelled with pride scorns to stoop, till God by his grace or judgments do lay it.

Why Do They Do It?

How comes it to pass that sinners so abuse God's patience with them?

Sin reigning in the ungodly, fear of wrath is their highest motive to good, and most forcible restraint from evil: and so when that restraint is taken off by the delay of execution again and again; the heart naturally goes to its own bias, and is like the wild ass's colt snuffing up the wind at her pleasure. The love of holiness for itself, and likeness to God, would prevent it.

They mistake the design of providence. They misinterpret the slow method of procedure with them (Ps. 50:21). The design of it is to lead them to repentance; but that they notice not. But they construe it, as if God approved of their ways, or had such a regard for them, that he will not be so angry with them, as one would make them believe: they cannot think that he is so very angry at their sin, while they prosper in it by his providence.

There is a root of atheism in the hearts of all men naturally, and it reigns in the ungodly: 'The fool has said in his heart, there is no God' (Ps. 14:1). Unless God be every now and then proving his being, providence, and justice to them, by his works of judgment on themselves; they are apt to forget him, and deny him. It is the interest of men wedded to their lusts, that there were not a God; or, if there be, that he were not such as the scripture represents him. So they are ready to entertain everything that may favour it.

The Lord often in that way carries on a holy hardening work. In which case, Satan and the evil heart conspire to this abuse.

Using the Truth

> That we need not to be surprised to see sinners escaping with one evil work fall into another, and so on; growing still more vile, the more outward favours are heaped on them. It is but a fulfilling of this scripture. Providence often has an odd aspect in our view, till we carry the matter to the Bible; and there we see it exactly answering the word.

> It is good for men to be under frequent rebukes of Providence. Affliction is sore, but it is the more safe lot (Ps. 119:71). In the one men are put in mind of their sins, in the other they are apt to forget both their God and themselves. It would be profitable for the afflicted to consider the wretched abuse the heart is ready to make of ease and prosperity.

> Slow vengeance will be sore vengeance, when it comes. For the longer it is a-coming, sin goes the deeper: the more God spares impenitents, the more they treasure up wrath against the day of wrath; the counts run on, and swell the more. So whether we consider it coming on in time or in eternity, the heavier will it be.

> Great is the corruption of human nature. See it here as in a glass, how the mercy and goodness of God are despised by the corrupt heart, that will not be drawn by such cords of love. See how it turns our good into poison, and that which should be for our welfare into a snare and trap. See it an ungrateful nature, apt to be insensible of the ties of gratitude to our best benefactor.

Do Not Test God's Patience

Take heed of abusing the patience of a long-suffering God, of turning his grace, goodness, and forbearance into wantonness, of your heart filling to do evil while God spares.

It Is Evil Behaviour

Consider the evil of it. There is in it an over-valuing of ourselves, as if we deserved not to be worse treated, and therefore were nothing obliged to our benefactor: 'They sacrifice to their net, and burn incense to their drag: because by them their portion is fat, and their meat plenteous' (Hab. 1:16). Men, who are not bettered by God's goodness, their hearts swell in pride, as patience is used towards them: 'They are not in trouble as other men:

239

neither are they plagued like other men. Therefore pride compasses them about as a chain: violence covers them as a garment' (Ps. 73:5-6).

An undervaluing of others whom providence does not treat so softly. Hence Job said, 'He that is ready to slip with his feet, is as a lamp despised in the thought of him that is at ease' (Job 12:5). How lightly do many that are at ease, look on the heavy things others suffer? They are as unconcerned with them, as if they were creatures of an inferior rank. Were men sensible of God's goodness, in his patience towards them, it would make them sympathize with others, wondering that it is not worse with themselves (2 Chron. 28:10).

A monstrous abuse of the creatures, and comforts of life (Hosea 2:8). The use of the creature was given to man, for his comfort indeed; but always in subserviency to the glory of God. But abusers of divine patience turn the weapons against God, which he has armed them with for his service: 'But Jeshurun waxed fat, and kicked: you are waxen fat, you are grown thick, you are covered with fatness; then he forsook God which made him, and lightly esteemed the Rock of his salvation' (Deut. 32:15). They are called adulterers and adulteresses because they bestow God's good gifts on their lusts (James 4:3-4). Hence the creation groans under the burden of the ungodly, evil-workers (Rom. 8:22).

A denying the due tribute to our Sovereign Lord and King. All that we have we hold of him, in the way of free mercy (Lam. 3:22). The king in his palace, and the beggar in his cottage, is God's tenant: our food and raiment, coarse or fine, with conveniencies of life, are given us of God. We can pay him nothing, but the tribute of praise in our lips and lives: and that is denied.

Hence, monstrous ingratitude, a sin of a deep dye, 'Do you thus requite the Lord, O foolish people and unwise? Is not he your father that has bought you? Has he not made you, and established you?' (Deut. 32:6). It is a devilish disposition of heart, that cannot be won with benefits; a base spirit, which good done them cannot engage. But abusers of mercies, the more God loads them with benefits, the more they load him with their provocations. Ah! Will men sin, because grace abounds? Will their hearts be filled in them to do evil, because the sentence against an evil work is not speedily executed?

Practically blasphemy, as if men should say, they are hired to be vile (Jer. 7:9-10). Abusers of the doctrine of the gospel, to licentiousness, make Christ the minister of sin: therefore abusers of the kind providence of God to that end, make God in his government of the world so. While heaven smiles in outward favours on men, and they use them so, the language of that practice is blasphemous.

Much atheism and contempt of God. It is a denial of his providence, as if he had no concern about human affairs (Ezek. 9:9). It makes a jest of his threatenings in his word, (2 Pet. 3:3-4). It misrepresents his holy nature (Ps. 50:21), or bids him defiance (Isa. 5:19), and throws off his yoke (Ps. 12:4).

It Is Highly Dangerous

Consider the danger of it. If you go on so you will make your recovery aye more and more hopeless (Jer. 6:29-30). Sin is a current, the farther it runs, the deeper it grows: and the more goodness men sin against, the more is their heart hardened, and their consciences seared. Withal it provokes God to give up with men, leave striving with them, and give them up to their lusts, and to the devil, to be hardened more.

If God has any thoughts of good towards you, it will make your recovery more difficult. Strong diseases must have strong remedies: and long abused patience will make broken bones, at best; if you be saved, it will be so as by fire. At best you are but laying up for bitter repentance: the more loose and licentious one is in an unconverted state, the more severe pangs and throes he will readily find in the new birth. Witness Manasseh and Paul.

Be it as it will, that patience will have an end; you will not sin on and God spare on very long. The coupling of these two will be broken, and God will show you that he will bear no longer with your abuse: 'For as the crackling of thorns under a pot, so is the laughter of the fool' (Eccles. 7:6). You will find God will awake to judgment, and wake you out of your dream; and you will either be his converts, or broken to pieces by him.

The breaking up of patience with you is likely to be very sudden and surprising (1 Thess. 5:2-3). So was it with the rich man (Luke 12:19-20). God bore long with the old world, but at length the deluge came on like a thunderclap, in the midst of their carnal mirth and jollity. God does it in just recompense of long abused patience.

Abused patience, when it breaks off, will burn to fury; and the longer God has delayed execution, the more severe will it be when it comes on (Lev. 26:28). The more a man has had in trust, his accounts will be found the greater and the harder to clear off, when once the creditors fall on him. It is most pleasing to the flesh, to live in ease and fullness; but the abuse of these will make a more fearful reckoning, than otherwise.

9

Execution – Slow but Sure

Though the execution be never so slow, it will be sure, against impenitent sinners, evil-workers.

An Unquashable Conviction

In what respects will the execution against impenitent sinners, evil-workers, be sure?

It will be sure, in respect of the full tale of their evil works: 'For God will bring every work into judgment, with every secret thing, whether it be good, or whether it be evil' (Eccles. 12:14). Neither the multitude of them, nor the long time they lie over unreckoned for, will cause any of them to be forgotten. But the ill works of the several periods of the sinner's life, will be charged home upon him exactly. For God keeps a register of all their evil works, a book that will be opened at the last day (Rev. 20:12); and has sworn that none of them will be forgotten (Amos 8:7).

The whole aggravations of their evil works (Jude 15). A just God will remember against impenitent sinners, the manner as well as the matter of their sins; the time, place, and other circumstances of their evil works, will be remembered against them. Their abused mercies, the light they rebelled against, the warnings from the word and providence they slighted, the effects their ill example had on others, the snares others were entangled therein by their means, will all be charged on them.

The conviction of their own consciences (Jude 15). Sinners now find ways to cloak and cover their evil works, to deny or mince them: and few will now suffer themselves to be admonished or reproved, but they have a great deal to say in their own defence; but the lying lips, and tongues that speak proudly, will then be put to silence (Matt. 22:12). The light of conscience will then be like broad day-light, that is now as the darkness of the night. It will convince them clearly of what will be laid to their charge, that they can no more deny it (John 8:9); and of the justice of God in proceeding against them (Ps. 50:6).

Just punishment brought on them for their evil works (1 Thess. 5:3). While God delays, men dream with Agag, that the bitterness of death is past: but they will find themselves deceived, as he when Samuel took the sword and hewed him in pieces before the Lord. They cannot escape the due demerit of their sin at length; but as the needle draws the thread after it, sin will draw wrath. Judgment is sin's shadow.

The correspondence there will be between their sin and punishment. God will write every ungodly sinner's sin in his punishment. Often it is so here with them, as in the case of Adonibezek (Judg. 1:7); but always so hereafter, as in the case of the rich man (Luke 16:19, 24). Hence the worm is said never to die; signifying the eternal remorse they will have for their evil works. And the degrees of punishment will be suited to the degrees of their sin. They that have committed many sins, will have many stripes.

The execution of the sentence is inevitable once patience is come to an end:

> Strive to enter in at the strait gate: for many, I say to you, will seek to enter in, and will not be able. When once the Master of the house is risen up, and has shut the door, and you begin to stand without, and to knock at the door, saying, Lord, Lord, open to us; and he will answer and say to you, I know you not whence you are (Luke 13:24-5).

The door of mercy may stand open long, but it will be shut at length. And then there is no more escaping:

1. Omniscience will find out the flier, and discover his most secret crimes, and overthrow all his defences: 'Neither is there any creature that is not manifest in his sight: but all things are naked, and opened to the eyes of him with whom we have to do' (Heb. 4:13). 'Whither will I go from your Spirit? Or whither will I flee from your presence?' (Ps. 139:7). There is no blinding of the eye of an omniscient judge.

2. Divine power will bring him under, and cause him to stand and receive the just reward of his deeds: 'He is wise in heart, and mighty in strength: who has hardened himself against him, and has prospered?' (Job 9:4). There will be no resisting of omnipotence: the stoutest sinner will be poured out like water before an angry God.

3. The divine severity will proceed over the belly of all entreaties, made out of time (Luke 13:24-5). They that slight mercy while God's time for it lasts, will get no mercy when God's time is out, and theirs is come.

The execution once on, will never be off; once begun, will never end (Mark 9:44). In hell the worm dies not, and the fire is not quenched. While God is, he will pursue the quarrel. The ungodly sin on as long as they are in the world, and live on as long as they will, they will not alter their course: and God will pursue them for ever, when once he has broke off.

No Last Minute Reprieve

That the execution against them will be sure appears from the inviolable regard God has to the honour of his holy law (Isa. 42:21). Sinners trample on it, slight its commands, and despise its threatenings; but God highly regards it, as that in which he has eminently expressed the holiness of his nature. If sinners then honour it not in the way of duty, it will be honoured upon them in a way of judgment. God's regard to his law may be seen clearly:

1. In the works of providence. As soon as sin entered into the world, and the law was broken, the face of providence on the world was quite changed. And it has blown continually since in the face of the creation less or more (Rom. 8:22). Often it has risen to violent storms, to avenge the quarrel of the dishonour of the holy law by sinners. Remember how, in the quarrel, Adam was driven out of Paradise, the world drowned by the flood, Sodom burnt, Jerusalem destroyed, with the many awful strokes brought on impenitent sinners in latter times.

2. In the work of redemption. God chose some from eternity to salvation: but being breakers of the law, they behoved to be redeemed, and the price paid to

the full reparation of the honour of the law. Christ the Son of God was their Redeemer; but that the law's honour might be seen to, he met with no sparing: 'He spared not his own Son, but delivered him up for us all' (Rom. 8:32). So God wrote his regard to the law in the salvation of his elect, and blood of his Son.

The truth and veracity of God insure the execution. He has said, he will do it: 'In the day that you eat thereof, you will surely die' (Gen. 2:17). His Son has intimated to us from heaven, that impenitent sinners will not escape: 'I tell you, No, but unless you repent, you will all likewise perish' (Luke 13:3). Every leaf of the scriptures almost, has something to this purpose: 'and has he said, and will he not do it? Or has he spoken, and will he not make it good?' (Num. 23:19). God's truth must either fail, or ungodly sinners be reckoned with at length.

The justice of God requires it: 'Shall not the Judge of all the earth do right?' (Gen. 18:25). Men may be unjust judges, but God cannot. He will give every transgression a just recompense of reward: for it is in his power to do it, and his nature requires it. He hates sin, and cannot but hate it; and therefore though he delay for a time, he will punish.

The constant conduct of providence hitherto confirms it. There have been multitudes of ungodly in the world; but may we not put the question, 'Who has hardened himself against him, and has prospered?' (Job 9:4). Some have indeed been long spared, but did they not at length either bow or break before him? What came of the giants in the old world, of Pharaoh, of Korah, Dathan, and Abiram?

These things happened for warnings to us. And if any have escaped during life, is there not sufficient evidence of execution on them in another world? As is evident from the case of the rich man (Luke 16).

The peremptory appointment of the day of general judgment, puts it out of question:

> And the times of this ignorance God winked at; but now commands all men everywhere to repent: because he has appointed a day in the which he will judge the world in righteousness, by that man whom he has ordained; of which he has given assurance to all men, in that he has raised him from the dead (Acts 17:30-31).

The Judge is named for that effect already, the commission to him for that end has passed the seals in his resurrection; it is to be general, all must be judged by him; yea the sentence against the ungodly is conceived already, 'Depart from me, you cursed, into everlasting fire, prepared for the devil and his angels.'

Using the Truth

To the ungodly, evil-workers

> Let not your impunity for the present, make you secure for the time to come; as is the case of the wicked man, 'He has said in his heart, I will not be moved: for I will never be in adversity' (Ps. 10:6). As sure as you think your mountain now stands, it may suddenly be overturned; yea it will assuredly, if you repent not. God is giving you space to repent: do not trifle and dream it away, lest you repent when it is too late.

> Let not your observation of the prosperity of other sinners, encourage and harden you in your sinful course: as it did those, 'And now we call the proud happy: yea, they that work wickedness are set up; yea, they that tempt God are even delivered' (Mal. 3:15). You have seen much of their sinful course, and of God's patience. But you have not seen the end of it yet: 'In the day will you make your plant to grow, and in the morning will you make your seed to flourish: but the harvest will be a heap in the day of grief, and of desperate sorrow' (Isa. 17:11). Many a day has begun fair, and held on long so, that has had a foul evening. And whatever you have observed of them, their prosperity in their ill course will be their end in bitter repentance, or in their destruction, or else the word of truth fails.

> Take the alarm in time, and flee from the wrath to come: 'Seek you the Lord while he may be found, call you upon him while he is near. Let the wicked forsake his way, and the unrighteous man his thoughts: and let him return to the Lord, and he will have mercy upon him; and to our God, for he will abundantly pardon' (Isa. 55:6-7). Know you cannot prosper to the end, in your loose and licentious ways. You must come to Christ by faith, and leave the world lying in wickedness; must break off your sins by repentance; or else you will perish. If you do it not, you will mind that you have been fairly warned, and lament for ever your slighting it.

To the godly

> Beware of entertaining any idol of jealousy in your heart, wherewith the Lord may be provoked against you. He is impartial in his judgments, and even his own will not escape: 'Who gave Jacob for a spoil, and Israel to the robbers? Did not the Lord, he, against whom we have sinned? For they would not walk in his ways, neither were they obedient to his laws' (Isa. 42:24). Though being in Christ you have shut the gulf as to condemnation, you may be severely chastised; and you may get broken bones for your transgressions, though you cannot lose your souls.

> Be not discouraged in the Lord's way, because in it you meet with many sore trials, while others that are far from it go at ease. The work-ox goes with the yoke on his neck, while the slaughter-ox is full fed. But the former is preserved, while the latter is slain and hewed in pieces.

To all

> Know that God is a holy jealous God. The way of sin is dangerous, and there will be no peace in the end of it.

> Let us prepare to meet our God in the way of his judgments. God's proceedings against the land are slow, but they are like to be sure and sore. He has made the earth to quake beneath us, shown his anger from the face of the heavens above us.

About this book

The contents of this book are taken from the sixth volume of *The Whole Works of the Late Reverend Thomas Boston of Ettrick*. They were first produced from manuscripts and pulpit notes. The text is unaltered apart from small changes to the English, with words such as 'unto' becoming 'to', and where the following features, designed to make the book more user-friendly, required minor changes:

1. Subheadings largely based on the original numeric structure, have been inserted. The contents pages include primary and secondary subheadings to aid navigation.

2. Sentences enumerating more than five or six items, lists of more than one sentence, selected notes, and his sections of application are broken off from the main text and displayed.

3. The style and placement of biblical references have been made consistent with modern practice and Roman numerals have been changed to Arabic.

These Puritan works are now available in the Christian Heritage imprint.

978-1-78191-108-2

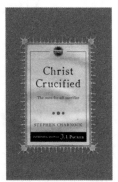

978-1-84550-976-7

978-1-84550-649-0

978-1-84550-650-6

978-1-84550-648-3

978-1-78191-107-5

978-1-84550-977-4

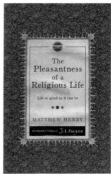

978-1-84550-651-3

978-1-84550-975-0

"a treat for anyone with healthy spiritual taste buds."
SINCLAIR B. FERGUSON

PURITAN
PORTRAITS

● ● ●

J. I. PACKER

ON SELECTED CLASSIC PASTORS
AND PASTORAL CLASSICS

978-1-84550-700-8

Puritan Portraits

J. I. Packer on Selected Classic Pastors and Pastoral Classics

J. I Packer

With characteristic ease of style, clarity of thought, and theological insight, Dr Packer introduces us to the life and thought of seven of the all-time masters of what one of them called 'the life of God in the soul of man.' Puritan Portraits is a treat for anyone with healthy spiritual taste buds.

Sinclair B. Ferguson,
Senior Minister, The First Presbyterian Church, Columbia, South Carolina

In an age of trendy fluff, here is solid food for the church and for the soul.

Carl R. Trueman,
Paul Woolley Professor of Historical Theology and Church History, Westminster
Theological Seminary, Philadelphia, Pennsylvania.

…simply no better tour guide for exploring Puritan faith and spirituality than J. I. Packer. Highly recommended!

Sam Storms,
Pastor, Bridgeway Church, Oklahoma City, Oklahoma

J. I. Packer can't wait to introduce us to the Puritans' rich theology and deep spirituality. J. I. Packer gives us profiles of John Flavel, Thomas Boston, John Bunyan, Matthew Henry, Henry Scougal, John Owen and Stephen Charnock and two closer portraits of William Perkins and Richard Baxter. J I Packer considers this head-line hitting holiness movement, their analytical thoroughness and literary legacy and the Puritan ideal for pastors. Come and join J. I. Packer as he introduces us to Puritan literature which he helps to bring alive for today's audience.

J. I. Packer is named by *Time* Magazine as one of the 25 most influential evangelicals alive. He is the Board of Governor's Professor of Theology at Regent College, Vancouver, BC, Canada.

Christian Focus Publications
publishes books for all ages

Our mission statement –

STAYING FAITHFUL
In dependence upon God we seek to impact the world through literature faithful to His infallible Word, the Bible. Our aim is to ensure that the LORD Jesus Christ is presented as the only hope to obtain forgiveness of sin, live a useful life and look forward to heaven with Him.

REACHING OUT
Christ's last command requires us to reach out to our world with His gospel. We seek to help fulfil that by publishing books that point people towards Jesus and help them develop a Christ-like maturity. We aim to equip all levels of readers for life, work, ministry and mission.

Books in our adult range are published in three imprints.

Christian Focus contains popular works including biographies, commentaries, basic doctrine and Christian living. Our children's books are also published in this imprint.

Mentor focuses on books written at a level suitable for Bible College and seminary students, pastors, and other serious readers. The imprint includes commentaries, doctrinal studies, examination of current issues and church history.

Christian Heritage contains classic writings from the past.

Christian Focus Publications Ltd,
Geanies House, Fearn, Ross-shire,
IV20 1TW, Scotland, United Kingdom
info@christianfocus.com
www.christianfocus.com